A PRACTICAL GUIDE TO

POPULAR
GARDEN
PLANTS

A PRACTICAL GUIDE TO
POPULAR
GARDEN
PLANTS

Bramley Books

Introduction

Most gardeners have favourite plants and though these may be exotic, intricately formed and rare, they are often so common that they are seen in practically every garden. Why a gardener favours a particular flower is one of life's mysteries, but their choice is often influenced by the memories that a particular flower evokes. Daffodils may bring back memories of romantic spring walks, while white lilac, which is often used in bridal bouquets, of a wedding day. Sometimes just the scent of a certain flower is enough to encourage a nostalgic smile. Other garden flowers may be cherished for more practical reasons, perhaps because they can be grown easily and create large drifts of colour in the garden.

Some flowers are so popular that they will be found in almost every garden. Roses, for example, have become something of an institution in English gardens. They are steeped in history and, whether they are old-fashioned roses or modern hybrids, bring a certain character to the garden. Lilies, which are also rich in history, are another popular garden plant and are frequently grown in borders as well as in pots on patios. Hyacinths and tulips – whose bulbs were so highly prized in the seventeenth century that a miller is reputed to have exchanged his mill for a prized bulb – are now widely grown, bringing the first splashes of colour to many a spring garden. This book looks at a wide spectrum of favourite garden plants and gives tips on how to get the very best from them.

© Marshall Cavendish 1995

Some of this material has previously appeared in the
Marshall Cavendish partwork **My Garden.**

4382
This edition published in 1997 by Bramley Books
Printed in Singapore
ISBN 1-85833-540-X

Contents

Colourful Anemones

The charming anemones bought from florists enjoy an enduring popularity, but they are just one member of a large, easy-going family of attractive garden flowers.

Photos Horticultural

When people think of anemones, they usually picture the cheerful and colourful blooms bought by the bunch at florists. These delightful plants have long been favourites because of their simple, cup-shaped flowers and the vibrant richness of their colours. However, there are many other types of anemone that are less well-known but just as stunning in their own way.

Hardy and versatile

All anemones are perennial; some grow from tubers or corms, others grow from creeping rhizomes. Some are frost hardy, which means that they will tolerate winter temperatures of −5°C/23°F, and some are fully hardy, which means that they can withstand temperatures as low as −15°C/5°F. Their perennial nature and general toughness make them an excellent choice for any garden.

Anemones are a versatile family. It is possible to have anemones of one sort or another blooming in your garden from early spring until well into autumn. There are even ones that will fill those awkward semi-shaded spots near hedges and walls. They can find homes in herbaceous borders, rock gardens, woodland areas or even on windowsills in or outside the house.

Colourful charmers

The most widely known anemones are varieties of the species *Anemone coronaria*. Their gorgeous colours make them instantly recognizable. These lovely plants come in two main types, the De Caen series and the St. Brigid series.

Both produce cup-shaped flowers. If you cut dead flowers back to soil level you may be rewarded with a succession of up to 20 flowers per plant, provided conditions are right. Just dig in plenty of well-rotted humus and follow the planting instructions carefully and you could get lots of flowers for your money.

Most garden centres sell the corms of De Caen and St. Brigid in packets of mixed colours. These include reds, deep blues or purples, various pinks and plain white. It is possible to buy named varieties in

The anemones commonly sold as cut flowers are the 'De Caen' series of Anemone coronaria (above). These vibrantly-coloured, single, spring blooms are available in named varieties, but are more commonly sold in packets of mixed colours.

Harry Smith Collection

Harry Smith Collection

PLANT PROFILE

Suitable site and soil Most species of anemones like humus-rich, well-drained soil and will thrive in full sun. Some prefer a semi-shaded position; others will even tolerate damp shade.

Cultivation and care Provided that you dig in plenty of humus before planting and the soil is free-draining, anemones require very little in the way of attention. *A. japonica* likes some lime in the soil. Dead-head *coronaria* varieties by cutting the stem at soil level for a succession of flowers. All forms are perennial although those growing from tubers may need replacing after a few years.

Propagation Tubers may be planted in late winter/early spring, in summer, or in the autumn, depending on when you want them to flower and the mildness of the winters in your area. Summer planting is only suitable in the mildest areas. Others may be propagated by division in spring, by seed sown when it is very fresh (usually midsummer) or by dividing rhizomes at the end of the season.

Pests and diseases Anemones are not particularly prone to pests and diseases but grey mould fungi may be a problem in wet/cold weather. Control by picking off infected leaves or, if it is a severe attack, use a fungicide. Powdery mildew may strike if conditions are hot and dry at the roots; water well and apply a mulch. Treat with a proprietary spray if necessary. The minute soil pests, symphylids, may be a nuisance in very mild, wet districts, chewing off the root hairs and destroying seedlings. In mature plants, lower leaves turn yellow and tops turn blue. If you know you have this problem, work HCH dust into the soil before planting. Greenfly may attack; use soapy water or a proprietary spray.

single colours. You may have to search around a bit to do this, but it will be worth it if you have a specific colour scheme in mind.

The main difference between De Caen and St. Brigid is size of flower. De Caen flowers are single, with between 5 and 8 large petals while those of the St. Brigid series are larger and variously described as double or semi-double, depending on whose catalogue you read; strictly, they are semi-double.

Varieties of *A. coronaria* are frost hardy and enjoy open, sunny sites and good drainage. Plant tubers in bold groups for the best effect. Height can be anything from 5-25cm/2-10in, depending on the variety. You will probably have to replace them in a few years as plants tend to get weak after a while.

Eastern promise

The Japanese anemone (variously known as *A.* × *hybrida* or *A. japonica*) is considered by many to be one of the most beautiful of garden plants.

Vigorous, fully hardy and with a branching habit, it blooms from late summer to early autumn, bridging that awkward gap between early and late bloomers. Flowers may be single, semi-double or double. 'Honorine Jobert' has lovely, pure white flowers

while others are various shades of pink. 'Max Vogel' tends towards mauve in colour and 'Prince Henry' is a deep, intensely rich pink.

Some varieties can grow to a height of 1.5m/5ft in favourable conditions and make good subjects for sites towards the back of the border. Others are shorter and can be placed to advantage in the centre or even at the front of a bed.

Japanese anemones look well backed by shrubs or planted with ornamental grasses, where their delicate flowers are shown off perfectly.

Sometimes described as doubles, the flowers of the 'St Brigid' series of A. coronaria *(top) are accurately called semi-double, despite their abundant petals, as their centres are open.*

PERFECT PARTNERS

Derek Gould

Derek Gould

Anemones' free-flowering nature is useful in schemes employing blocks of colour. Here, A. blanda *'White Splendour' combines dramatically with red tulips.*

Easily propagated in late autumn from root cuttings, they do well in partial shade and are good subjects for chalky or limy soils. Choose your site carefully; they tend to spread rather freely.

Small treasures

Varieties of *A. blanda* are small (height 5-10cm/4-6in) and fully hardy. They grow from knobbly tubers and produce star-shaped flowers with narrow petals in early spring. 'White Splendour' enjoys full sun, good drainage and humus-rich soil. 'Radar' has deep carmine flowers and will tolerate partial shade. 'Atrocaerulea' has deep blue flowers and likes good drainage and partial shade.

Anemone blanda varieties are easily propagated by dividing tubers when the leaves have died back in early winter. They also seed themselves freely. All varieties look good planted at the edge of mixed or herbaceous borders.

Shady characters

There are several species of anemone that will take to life in shaded and moist areas. *A. nemorosa* varieties are commonly known as wood anemones because they thrive in woodland conditions. This means partial or dappled shade and rich, well-rotted leaf mould at the roots. Such conditions also tend to be on the damp side.

There are several varieties to choose from, the most popular being the simple, star-

Harry Smith Collection

RECOMMENDED VARIETIES

- *A. coronaria.* De Caen Series bear single flowers and St. Brigid Series larger ones. Both come in bright colours including white, cerise, blue/purple and red. Good named varieties include 'Mr Fokker' (deep bluish purple) and 'Hollandia' (fiery red).
- *A. blanda.* Varieties include 'Atrocaerulea' (dark blue), 'Pink Star' and 'Charmer' (pink) and 'Radar' (magenta). For a clear white with a pale yellow centre, choose 'White Splendour'.
- *A. × hybrida* or *A. japonica.* 'Bressingham Glow' (semi-double rosy-red). 'Hadspen Abundance' (rose pink) is a newcomer and is very free flowering. 'Honorine Jobert' (white, single, with green centre surrounded by a ring of orange stamens) is an old favourite.
- *A. nemorosa* (wood anemone). 'Allenii' and 'Robinsoniana' both have star-shaped, lavender-blue flowers. 'Vestal' (white double) and 'Wilks' Giant' (large white single).
- *A. sylvestris* (snowdrop windflower) 'Macrantha' (scented white flowers).

Photos Horticultural

Tania Midgley

UNUSUAL HOUSEPLANTS

It is possible to grow *A. coronaria* as houseplants and to be rewarded by up to six months of flowers.

Plant up to five tubers in a 20cm/8in pot in good quality, loam-based compost. Keep the compost on the dry side of moist until the plants sprout.

Place plants in a cool (7-16°C/45-60°F), dry and well-ventilated position. Provide plenty of light, although young plants should be protected from full sun.

Water established plants twice weekly; more often in very hot weather. Do not spray the foliage as this will encourage fungal diseases. Once the plants are established, feed every ten days with a liquid feed.

Remove dead flowers at soil level to encourage new buds to form. When flowering is finished and no flower stems are visible, allow the foliage to die back and plant the tubers out in the garden. Do not try to grow the same tubers in a pot the following year; they will only produce weak specimens.

'Honorine Jobert' (above left) exemplifes the classic simplicity of Japanese anemones (A. × hybrida syn A. japonica of gardens).

The wood anemone (A. nemorosa) offers a carpet of foliage set off by star-shaped flowers in spring. The species is white, but 'Robinsoniana' (left) is a pale lavender.

Strong colours are a feature of all A. coronaria varieties. Perhaps the most startling of all is the hot, vivid scarlet of 'Hollandia' syn. 'His Excellency' (above), which positively leaps from the cool green of its deeply divided foliage.

The buttercup-yellow A. ranunculoides (right) thrives in woodland conditions, and grows a little taller than A. nemorosa.

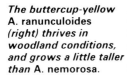

Harry Smith Collection

Many excellent garden varieties have been developed from the wild wood anemone (A. nemorosa). One of the best is 'Vestal' (right), a pure white double. All wood anemones hug the ground – few are taller than 15cm/6in – and make a good show in dappled shade.

The Japanese anemone (Anemone x hybrida), which blooms from late summer to early autumn, is considered one of the most beautiful garden plants. Some varieties produce delicate flowers that are a deep, intense pink colour (facing page).

Photos Horticultural

The Pasque flower (below), once part of the anemone genus, has been reclassified as Pulsatilla vulgaris. It also comes in red, pink and white.

shaped, lavender-blue 'Allenii' and 'Robinsoniana'. 'Vestal' is white and has double flowers; 'Wilks' Giant' (also sold as 'Wilks' White') is larger and single. All wood anemones have a creeping, carpeting habit and grow from rhizomes.

To increase stock, divide the rhizomes when the leaves die back. Blooms appear in spring and early summer and reach a height of about 15cm/6in and a spread of 30cm/12in or more.

A. sylvestris will also thrive in partial or dappled shade. Unlike the wood anemone, however, it likes a well-drained soil. The lovely, delicate white flowers are attractively scented and appear in spring and early summer.

This beauty has a carpeting habit and can be invasive, so pick your site well. Look out for the variety called 'Macrantha', which grows to a height and spread of 30cm/12in.

A. ranunculoides is different from the others in that its spring flowers resemble buttercups and are a deep, rich yellow. It enjoys damp, woodland conditions and has a spreading habit. Height and spread reach 20cm/8in.

A. × lipsiensis, also known as *A. × seemannii*, is a low growing, carpeting variety that enjoys partial shade and good drainage. It grows to about 15cm/6in tall, with a spread of 30cm/12in, and produces a profusion of pale yellow flowers in spring.

WHAT'S IN A NAME?

If you have been searching the catalogues for the Pasque flower (also known as the flower of Easter) under the name of *A. pulsatilla*, you may have been disappointed. It underwent a name change a while back and became *Pulsatilla vulgaris.*

Anemone or not, it is gorgeous and deserves a place in the garden. Its purple or white flowers appear in spring and are followed by seed heads that are lovely in their own right.

Just to confuse you still further, *A. hepatica* is also known as *Hepatica nobilis* and is well worth investigating. It has semi-evergreen, leathery leaves and comes in lilac-mauve, white or pink. It flowers in spring and enjoys damp shady places.

Don Wildridge

Graceful Petunias

If ever a plant deserved its popularity, it is the petunia. Easy to grow and readily available, it comes in a palette of colours to brighten up your summer displays.

Andrew Lawson

Pat Brindley

There are many hardy and half-hardy annuals from which to choose when you are planning your summer flower beds, window boxes, tubs and hanging baskets; so many, in fact, that a trip to the garden centre can leave you bewildered and spoilt for choice. There is one plant, however, that deserves to be right at the top of your list: the versatile and much-loved petunia.

Whatever colour scheme you choose, there will be petunias to fit the bill. If you want subtlety there are pastel shades, including the palest pinks, blues and creams. If you want a really rich effect, on the other hand, pick deep purples and maroons, with perhaps a

Petunias come in a wide variety of shades and forms. Try a carpet of 'Frenzy Mixed' (above) with its harmonious shades of red, pink and violet and its clear, simple shape. To combine form with colour choose a double with ruffled petals like the 'Giant Victorious Mixed' (above right).

stripe of pure white as a striking contrast.

For a real riot of colour, choose varieties that are positively gaudy, such as 'Razzle Dazzle' (a mixture of red, deep rose, deep blue and crimson flowers, each with white stripes). On the other hand, you may prefer to stick to the pure primary colours of bright blue, red and yellow. The list is endless and is being extended every year.

As if the choice of colours were not enough, the splendid petunia also offers a number of different forms.

Take your pick

Choose multiflora varieties for plants which flower repeatedly. 'Dwarf Resisto Mixed' is a multiflora that thrives in poor summer weather conditions. 'Star Joy' is a rich rose colour with a pure white star in the centre of each of its many blooms. 'Summer Sun' is a glorious yellow and there are many more multiflora varieties. Take time to browse through some catalogues, before you make your selection.

The grandiflora varieties have larger but fewer flowers than multifloras. The 'Super-

PLANT PROFILE

Suitable site and soil: an open, sunny site for preference but petunias will tolerate some shade. Ordinary soil, not waterlogged. Particularly suited to growing in containers, where you should use ordinary potting compost. Do not overfeed or put in an over-rich compost as this will encourage plants to produce foliage growth at the expense of flowers.

Planting: plant out in late spring or early summer, after all danger of frost has passed, 20-30cm/8-12in apart in borders or beds. May be packed closer in containers. Water in dry weather until well established. Cut stems back if they become too straggly and dead-head regularly to prolong flowering season.

Propagation: germinate seeds in gentle heat, 18-24°C/65-75°F in early spring. They take between 7-21 days to appear. Make sure pots and trays are clean, to avoid diseases like damping-off. Use moist, good quality seed compost. Sprinkle seed onto the compost and firm in; do not cover with soil. Place in a propagator or cover pots with cling film and place on a sunny windowsill. Keep moist.

Pests and diseases: vulnerable to aphids, cucumber mosaic virus and tomato spotted wilt virus. Susceptible to rot if planted too close together in excessively wet conditions.

Available types: too many named varieties to list. Types include multiflora, grandiflora, doubles, frilled or ruffled, veined or laced, bi-coloured, star or picotee, and cascading. Colours include white, cream, various pinks from very pale to very dark, blues, purples, reds, yellow and orange. Height can vary from 15cm/6in to 45cm/18in. Look out also for those bred specifically for growing in hanging baskets where cascading types look particularly well. If you particularly want a specific variety, you may have to go to a specialized nursery as many garden centres and shops stock only a limited number of varieties.

Eric Crichton

Andrew Lawson

Petunias make a good edging plant at the front of a bed. If the other plants are colour-coordinated, a single colour like the deep pink 'Resisto Rose' (above) may be the most effective, but the petunia's vast variety of shapes and colours offers endless scope.

'Purple Pirouette' with its violet and white ruffled petals (below) is one of the most striking of the double petunias. It looks good on its own or in combination with other petunias or bedding plants in a mixed display.

Introduce a note of drama to your borders or containers with the dramatic red and white colouring of 'Red Star' (left). This variety looks particularly good when combined with plain red or white petunias or with other white bedding plants.

Petunia 'Frenzy Red Vein' (below) is a single flower whose delicate rose-pink colour is subtly enhanced by darker veins. Grow it on its own or mixed with some of the other pink varieties in a single-colour bed, or try two or three plants in a single pot on the patio or window ledge.

Pat Brindley

Pat Brindley

magic' series comes in single colours such as coral, mid-blue, light blue and orange. 'Crimson Star', another grandiflora, is a deep crimson colour with a white star. Again, the sheer number of varieties makes it impossible to list them all but whichever you choose, you will get plenty of flowers per plant. Petunias always give you good returns and value for money.

A feast of colour

Double petunias have large, carnation-like flowers. They look good in pots arranged in groups around the garden and patio. 'Bonanza Mixed' has frilly edges and 'Double Fanfare Mixed' some very beautiful bi-colours. 'Purple Pirouette' is a rich violet double with pure white ruffled edges, and 'Red Bouquet' is a fringed double with bright scarlet blooms.

Bi-colours come in both sin-

Photos Horticultural

Create instant colour wherever you need it in the garden with a portable petunia in a pot or other container. This lovely example (above) is the single 'Express Blush Pink'.

Harry Smith

GARDEN NOTES

TAKING A CHANCE

If you want to pick and choose your petunias, you can buy seed by mail order. Seedlings are also available by post but the range is more limited and orders have to be placed early in the year. If you are willing to take pot luck, the easiest way to achieve a display of petunias is to buy them as bedding plants – most garden centres stock plenty of dependable varieties such as the Resisto range. It is also worth looking in greengrocers and florists, but check the quality carefully before buying.

gle and double forms. Some have central stars, while picotee varieties have white edges. For added beauty, choose those with frilled or ruffled edges. There are many varieties of bi-colours; among the best are 'Razzle Dazzle', 'Picotee Ruffled Mixed', 'Blue Frost' (violet blue, white edge), 'Star Fire' (scarlet and white), 'Crimson Star', 'Star Joy' (rose with white star) and 'Cherry Tart' (deep rose and white).

To make the job of choosing

there are also the veined varieties, known as 'lacy' petunias. 'Plum Purple' is a rich purple-crimson with a deep plum coloured throat and veins, while 'Lacy Sails' is a soft blue with a deep blue throat and veins. There are also mixed varieties. Look out for 'Kaleidoscope Mixed' and 'Daddy Mixed', if you want a good mix of colours.

For baskets and window boxes there are some specially bred, cascading varieties. Look out for 'Ruby Cascade', 'Super Cascade Lilac' (also sold as 'Birthday Celebrations') or the blush pink variety 'Super Cascade Blush Improved'.

Summer bedding is all about profusion. This is especially true of tubs, window boxes and hanging baskets. Containers or beds with just a few isolated plants can be a forlorn sight. This is where the petunia comes into its own. Given the right conditions it will branch out beautifully, its leaves and blooms filling the same space as several lesser plants.

Perfect planting

Once you have made your purchases, you are ready to begin planting in late spring or early summer. Do not plant out whilst there is any risk of frost.

Clear the site of weeds and other debris. If the soil is very poor, a light dusting of an all-purpose, organic fertilizer such as blood, fish and bone should be raked in. Petunias do not respond well to over-feeding as it leads to the production of leaves at the expense of the flowers.

For the best effect, plant petunias in fairly large groups, perhaps in clusters at the front of a border. They should be planted 20-30cm/8-12in apart but may be packed closer together if you are putting them in containers.

Whether you buy bedding plants or grow your own petunias from seed, the aftercare is the same. Remove dead flower heads immediately to encourage a succession of blooms lasting all summer long. Petunias are inclined to attract aphids so it is important that you keep an eye on them and treat them at the first sign of insect infestation.

If you are fairly diligent about these things your plants will flower happily from early summer until the first hard frosts of autumn.

Andrew Lawson

Petunias are ideal for growing in a variety of locations, including window boxes (right) or raised beds (below). Grow them on their own or mix them with other plants such as ivy, fuchsia and geranium for a striking and long-lasting display. Choose both upright and trailing varieties for best effect. A small bed of petunias (bottom) brightens up a corner of the patio perfectly.

Peter McHoy

Tania Midgley

SAFE AND STRONG

● Check your plants carefully before buying to ensure strong, healthy specimens.
● Handle petunias gently and shelter them from strong winds, as the stems tend to snap fairly easily, though they do recover quickly from such accidents.
● Remove dead flower heads regularly, especially after heavy rain, as flowers tend to become pulpy when soaked with water.

GROWING TIPS

Summer Bedding Plants

Bringing home a trayful of new plants for your garden can be so exciting. Here's how to plant them for maximum effect and long-lasting colour

John Hooton/The Garden Picture Library

Bedding plants are so called because that is the way in which they are used: they are 'bedded out' for display, another term for planting. The plants are mainly hardy annuals, capable of surviving outdoors all year round and half-hardy annuals.

Splashes of colour

The main use of bedding plants is to introduce colour to the garden throughout the summer, and as they are a temporary addition you can change the display every year.

Nearly all summer bedding plants have plenty of brightly coloured blooms, which is why they are so popular. They transform a flower bed into an attractive bank of colour, and just a few added to a border of shrubs works wonders.

So versatile, bedding plants

Summer glory: a stunning and easy-to-achieve show of colour. Tall bedding dahlias in bright hues provide a backdrop for a mass of busy Lizzies in boldly clashing shades of pink and red.

need not be restricted to beds and borders, many grow happily in containers such as patio tubs, window boxes and hanging baskets.

Visual effects

Your local nursery or garden centre should have a wide variety of plants to whet your appetite, with contrasts in colour, texture, shape and size. You may like to arrange your

PLANNING A BORDER

An informal bedding scheme (above) is created by grouping several different varieties of bedding plants in random clusters; while a formal look (below) is achieved by setting colours together and using the silver-leafed cineraria as a feature plant.

CREATING A LOOK

It is a good idea to think about what sort of look you want to achieve with your new bedding plants *before* you start digging and planting. Put the plants out on the earth while they are still in their containers and move them around into different positions to give you an indication of the final effect. As a general rule, tall plants look best at the back, medium ones set mid-way, and small ones at the front where they will not be hidden. Use the list (right) to help you plan your scheme. All the plants listed are popular, easily available varieties.

Photos Horticultural

PICK OF THE PLANTS

Tall
aster
bells of Ireland (moluccella)
Canterbury bell (campanula)
clarkia
dahlia – bedding type
schium
fuchsia
love-lies-bleeding (amaranthus)
lupin (lupinus)
salpiglossis
summer cypress (kochia)
sweet William (dianthus)
tobacco plant (nicotiana)
wallflower (cheiranthus)

Paul Felix

Medium
African daisy (arctotis)
begonia – fibrous rooted
busy Lizzie (impatiens)
calendula (pot marigold)
cineraria (senecio)
coleus
cosmos (cosmea)
bellis perennis
dwarf sweet pea (lathyrus)
gazania
geranium (pelargonium)
love-in-a-mist (nigella)
nemesia
petunia
phlox
reseda (mignonette)
salvia
snapdragon (antirrhinum)
Star of the Veldt (dimorphotheca)
tagetes (African marigold)
zinnia

Short
alyssum
Californian poppy (eschscholzia)
candytuft (iberis)
dianthus – bedding
dwarf busy Lizzie (impatiens)
flower floss (ageratum)
lobelia
pansy
tagetes (French marigold)

plants quite formally, in tidy rows, or grouped informally around hardy perennials, shrubs and shrub roses.

Bedding plants really do look at their most glorious when displayed to show off their vibrant colours – it never seems to matter that 'clashing' colours sit side by side. Shocking pink, hot red and brilliant orange can look wonderful together in the flower bed.

If you want a less brazen effect, however, bedding plants look equally attractive when used as part of a more restrained colour scheme: pink and white is a popular combination, as is yellow and blue, or you could limit yourself to shades of one colour, against a backdrop of green shrubbery.

Buying for borders
In your enthusiasm to fill your garden with bright new plants, do not be tempted to buy at the first opportunity. Although bedding plants are sold by market traders, florists and some supermarkets, it is generally advisable to purchase them from a garden centre or nursery. Wherever you buy, it must have the proper environment and facilities for

John Glover/The Garden Picture Library

GARDENERS' TERMS

Annuals – plants that will only last a season.

Biennials – plants which flower in their second season, then die.

Half-hardy annuals – annuals that cannot withstand frost.

Hardy annuals – annuals that can withstand a moderate frost.

Perennials – plants which live longer than two years.

Tender – liable to be damaged by frost. A tender plant should be brought indoors while there is a danger of frost.

Harry Smith Collection

The clash of orange, red, white and purple works well in this border (left). The different flowers – alyssum (white), lobelia (blue), salvia (red) and French marigolds (orange) – are planted in blocks, rather than being allowed to intermingle, making each colour more pure and intense. The vivid green leaves of the salvia and marigolds add an equally stunning fifth colour to the display.

keeping the plants in good condition.

Summer bedding plants are generally available to buy from mid-spring through to early summer. Bear in mind they must not be planted out until danger of frost is over, which is late spring in warmer areas and early summer in colder places. If you have no facilities for holding plants until planting time (for example, a frost-free greenhouse or garden frame) then do not buy them until you are ready to plant.

Small bedding plants, like pansies, are often sold in trays

Using differences in height and colour to the full – the tallish African marigolds stand over a strip of low-lying lobelia. The bold yellow pompons of the marigolds (below) contrast in colour and form with the edging carpet of sprawling mauve lobelia.

GARDEN NOTES

PLANTING DISTANCES

Before planting out water each plantlet, preferably the night before – but do not water the bed or planting will be a very sticky business.

The distance at which to plant will depend on the final size of the plants you have chosen. If planting in rows, stagger each row for the best effect. As a rough guide, use the list (left) to help you:

- small, slow growers: space about 15cm (6in) apart
- medium-sized plants: space about 23-30cm (9-12in) apart
- large plants: space about 30-38cm (12-15in) apart

of 24 plants, though smaller quantities can be purchased in strips. Larger plants, such as pelargoniums, are usually sold singly in plastic or fibre pots.

Garden centres also sell ready-planted plastic containers, each with several plants coming into flower, which do not need planting out. They are simply placed in patio tubs or other ornamental containers to give an instant splash of colour.

Planning a scheme

A traditional summer bedding scheme, which is still popular today, consists of the main flower planted over a large area to form a colourful carpet: for instance, begonias, dorotheanthus or alyssum.

A few taller plants to give

19

PLANTING YOUR SUMMER BEDDING PLANTS

1 Before you start any digging or planting, assemble everything that you need: plants, peat, bone meal, watering can, tools and gloves.

2 Clear the area set aside for new plants by digging out any spent ones and removing weeds and their roots from the soil.

3 Starting at the back of the bed, use trowel to dig holes just bigger than the root balls of each plant. Space holes according to size of plant.

Simon Hay

5 To remove each plant, turn the pot upside-down, supporting the plant between your fingers, and tap the base or gently squeeze the pot.

6 Position the plant in its hole and check that the roots are not bent or cramped before replacing soil. Firm soil around the plant with your hands.

7 If the plants were grown in polystyrene trays, separate them by gently pulling apart the roots. Plant these as before (step 6).

FEEDING FLOWERS

Preparing beds and borders with the right balance of food will ensure a beautiful show of flowers all summer long. Bone meal is an organic fertilizer that releases its goodness slowly, so is specially good for shrubs and other slow-growing plants. Growmore is a general purpose fertilizer which acts more quickly than bone meal, but is suitable for annuals. Autumn is the ideal time for feeding soil with bone meal, but as bedding plants have fine root systems, springtime is perfectly adequate. Work the fertilizer into the top few inches of soil. Do not apply when the surface is dry.

Susie Johns

GARDEN NOTES

height to the scheme, generally with attractive foliage, are planted at random in this carpet, contrasting with it in colour, texture and shape. These are known as dot plants, or feature plants, a typical example being silver-leaved cineraria. The bed can be given a low contrasting edging, if desired, such as sweet alyssum, ageratum or lobelia.

If you want to plant a long border which is viewed from the front only, you may prefer to arrange the various flowers in bold informal groups. Set the tallest ones at the back, medium-height plants in the centre and short plants at the front. There is no need to stick rigidly to this rule: to avoid a regimented effect, you can occasionally extend groups of tall and short plants towards the centre of the border.

Getting good results

Most summer bedding plants should be grown in a sunny position, although there are a few which will succeed in partial shade.

They grow in any type of garden soil provided it is well drained and not prone to lying wet over the winter. The soil should be reasonably fertile but not over-rich. Once a year, before buying and planting

Before planting your bedding plants, sprinkle a fine layer of bone meal into each hole and work it in ly with a garden rake.

After all the plants are in place, hoe the soil around them to erase any footprints. Water the plants well a watering can with a fine rose.

BORDER PROBLEMS

Q My summer bedding plants grew very well but produced few flowers. Do they need feeding?

A It sounds like you may have added too much fertilizer already. Follow the instructions on the packet carefully.

Q My bedding plants flowered well initially, but then produced very few blooms. Why?

A You probably didn't remove the dead flowers from the plants often enough. Remove them regularly to encourage flowering.

Q My summer bedding plants flowered beautifully but now the flowers are becoming mouldy. What did I do wrong?

A You might have over-watered. Water new plants daily until they start to grow, then only when dry.

WHAT WENT WRONG?

David Russell/The Garden Picture Library

A white begonia and a mauve and white fuchsia (above) make a very pretty match. Begonias are probably the 'ultimate' bedding plant. Easy to care for, they flower profusely all summer and come in virtually any colour.

There is no restriction on where to use your bedding plants. They work equally well in pots or tubs and in flower beds. If you use pots, do make sure they have adequate drainage, use a proper planting medium (not garden soil) and remember to water and feed the plants regularly.

summer bedding, give the bed a light dressing of general purpose fertilizer, following the instructions on the pack, and lightly rake it into the surface.

Bedding plants are especially useful in new gardens which probably have a great deal of bare earth that needs to be covered quickly. They will give a good display of instant colour while you are doing some more long-term planning.

If your garden has just a few shrubs in it, use bedding plants to fill the spaces in between. Be sure to buy enough – over-planting looks better than under-planting, and helps to keep the weeds at bay, too.

FLOWERING PERIODS

Plan this year's display with reference to the chart below. Choose plants from the same colour band for planning simultaneous flowering or from different colour bands for consecutive flowering.

	MAY	JUNE	JULY	AUG	SEPT	OCT
ageratum						
alyssum						
antirrhinum						
calendula						
Canterbury bell						
Californian poppy						
cosmos						
dahlia						
dianthus						
dimorphotheca						
fuchsia						
candytuft						
clarkia						
busy Lizzie						
sweet pea						
lobelia						
tobacco plant						
petunia						
phlox						
nigella						
zinnia						
tagetes						

Note: All plants will be cut down by the first severe frost and weather will affect flowering.

Herbaceous Perennials

Lovely herbaceous perennials are the backbone of many gardens, providing long-term colour and blending well with annuals and existing shrubs. Needing the minimum of day-to-day maintenance, they are every gardener's dream.

Herbaceous perennials are hard-working, decorative plants that can generally be left undisturbed for many years. Once you have planted a selection of them you can sit back and enjoy the display with just the minimum of maintenance in the future.

The term 'perennial' is the name for a large group of very diverse plants that live for many seasons. You do not have to replace them or sow fresh seeds each year. Most of them take a rest from above-ground activity in winter, but when they spring into action in the growing season they provide a fine display of colour.

Herbaceous perennials are essential foundation plants in a garden as they provide much ornamental value for relatively little outlay. Most are tolerant of average conditions, but if you have a particularly dry or damp garden it is wise to choose those that will suit it.

Herbaceous perennials come in a range of shapes and sizes and differing flower colours, but their general behaviour is similar. They live for many seasons, producing flowers with consistent vigour, and in autumn most of them lose their stems and leaves. Underground, their root systems continue to live and many increase in size, spreading into clumps from the roots.

Garden value

Perennials are great value because they have long flowering periods. They come in a wide range of heights and are therefore versatile plants in any garden layout. They are relatively inexpensive to buy and they grow in size, providing you with extra plants over the years. Some herbaceous perennials form clumps and mats of vegetation that make good ground cover in a border, suppressing weed growth.

Some border perennials have green leaves during winter and these are the ones that will fill the gaps in the garden left by perennials that die back. Hellebores, including Christmas rose, have flowers and leaves through the year. Epimediums, too, hold their lovely autumn leaves until spring when delicate flowers dance above the new foliage.

Reliability

For gardeners the main attraction of herbaceous perennials is their general reliability and adaptability to a wide range of garden conditions.

In spring, when the soil is beginning to warm up and the growing season begins, herbacious perennials are on sale at garden centres, but they hardly look their best at this stage. All you can see in the pot is a few shoots and a clump of leaves. It is hard to believe

A border of herbaceous perennials, showing the variety of height and form that can be achieved. In the foreground are low-growing, mauve asters. In the centre is bright red montbretia. At the back are hollyhocks in two colours and the tall spikes of bear's breeches (Acanthus).

GARDEN NOTES

PLANTING OUT FROM POTS

Container-grown plants can be put out at any time of the year but between spring and autumn is usually the best time. Dig a hole sufficiently deep and wide to allow a full spread of the root system. For a large plant, mix some moist peat and some bonemeal with the soil in the planting hole. Ease out the roots from the pot, keeping the soil ball as complete as possible, and set in position. Depress the soil around the plant slightly to help it collect moisture, and water.

that this Cinderella will turn into a choice garden plant. In autumn, also a good planting time, there is little to see on most herbaceous perennials.

Are they hardy?

Most herbaceous perennials are hardy and will survive the winter without any frost protection. A few, such as red hot pokers, may need the crown

protecting in cold areas, with a layer of straw or bracken, or even a layer of weathered ash. Just a few, like dahlias, are tender and will be killed by frost; these must be lifted and given winter protection (as stored tubers in the case of dahlias), then replanted the following year.

From autumn to early spring is a good time to take root cuttings. Pot them up and keep them frost-free. Plant them out next autumn.

Some people feel that perennials leave too many gaps in winter when the majority die back. You can minimize this by clever planting with a few that do not die back, or with spring bulbs and winter flowering perennials. Today, most perennials are planted into mixed borders rather than in borders solely devoted to perennials, so gaps are not likely to be too noticeable. One of the

CHOICE PERENNIALS

- *Hellebores* grow to about 60cm/2ft and flower in winter or spring. Leave them undisturbed if possible. Hardy and evergreen.
- *Pulmonaria* (lungwort) has speckled foliage, is evergreen and hardy, flowers in early spring to early summer, does well in shade and is good ground cover. A useful front of border plant.
- *Sedum spectabile* has fleshy leaves and flowers late in autumn. It does well in hot and dry conditions and makes good ground cover in the middle of a border.
- *Aquilegia* (columbine) is not always very vigorous but is easy to replace with seedlings. The flowers are very graceful.
- *Rudbeckia* makes a splash of strong colour in late autumn and does well in sunny or shady sites.
- *Dianthus*, (which includes pinks and border carnations) provides a good show at the front of a border.
- *Lupins, hollyhocks* and *delphiniums* are favourite choices for the back of a border, or to give an island bed height. They need staking and may need replacing if they lose their flowering vigour.
- *Crocosmia* (montbretia) provides orange or red flowers in late summer. It will need dividing as it spreads quickly.
- *Japanese anemones* are excellent border perennials, providing dainty pink or white flowers on long stems that are self-supporting.

Photos Horticultural

Two choice perennials that will add colour to any flower bed. The bright pink of Sedum spectabile 'Autumn Joy' (above) and the bi-coloured flowers of the aptly-named Dianthus 'Snowfire' (below) which can be grown as an annual.

pleasures of these plants is the discovery of new shoots and leaves starting into growth after a dormant period.

Height and shape

When you decide to plant perennials there are a number of

Collections/Patrick Johns

factors you need to consider. First you should choose plants to suit your particular colour plans. Knowing their eventual height and shape is also important. If a plant is going to spread into a large space, it is no use planting anything too close to it. On the other hand, you do not want unsightly gaps in the soil, so spread is a necessary dimension to know.

Perennials vary greatly in height. Some, including delphiniums, traditional border giants, grow to 1.5m/5ft or more. They should be planted at the back of a border. There are many perennials that grow to medium heights (between 90cm/3ft and 1.2m/4ft), including Japanese anemones and day lilies *(Hemerocallis)*. Then come the vast majority that are up to 60cm/2ft high. For the front of a border or for growing on rockeries there are many perennials that do not grow taller than 15cm/6in, but they spread out wide to form ground-covering mats of flowers and leaves.

Good company
Perennials used to be planted in traditional one-sided borders that backed onto walls or hedges. Although glorious in the summer growing season, they were a depressing sight in winter. Today, perennials are usually combined with shrubs, bulbs and bedding plants in mixed borders that can give all-year pleasure.

Island beds, that can be seen from all angles, are popular for perennial plantings. Such beds offer all round light and good airflow. They are often very informal in style. Remember, though, when planting such a bed, that it will be seen from all directions. You can avoid using stakes by selecting varieties that are strong enough to support themselves, or will prop each other up.

Where to plant
The best site for most perennials is an open sunny position where their leaves can have as much light as possible. This makes it easier for them to make the food necessary for growth and flower production.

They need a well-drained soil but will want watering in extremely hot conditions. There should be a good flow of air around the perennial border to avoid a build up of pests

and diseases. However, exposed and windy sites are not suitable for these ornamental plants. The best soil to grow a wide range of perennials in is a medium loam that has been enriched with well-rotted compost or fertilizer. Whether you plant two or ten perennials in a border, they will all be competing for the sun, moisture, air and soil — so you should ensure that there is enough to go round when you plant them out. Space them out well.

General care
Although herbaceous perennials are not particularly demanding plants, they do need

The show of colour produced by an imaginative planting of herbaceous perennials in a mixed border (above) can be quite stunning. This picture was taken in late summer when the chosen flowers were at their best. They contrast pleasingly in height, form and colour with the clumps of ornamental grasses.

Almost anything that will keep the frost away can be used to protect delicate perennials. Here (below) dry leaves and stems are being placed on a wire frame over the crowns.

Photos Horticultural

Marshall Cavendish

Marshall Cavendish

PROJECT   DIVIDING PERENNIALS

Every three or four years you should rejuvenate perennials by lifting them in autumn and dividing them. When the plant is out of the ground, place it on a sheet of plastic and use two forks to lever it apart. Replant the sections of the root on the outer edge of the plant. Add a little slow release fertilizer and water them in. In spring you will have the bonus of extra plants.

The older roots at the centre of the plant will be less vigorous (producing fewer leaves and blooms if left to grow) and should be discarded.

some care and attention. You will need to feed your perennials with a general compound fertilizer in early spring when growth begins, and then again in mid-summer.

A mulch of organic material soon after the first feed helps to conserve moisture and discourages weeds. Apply the mulch thickly to a depth of 7.5cm/3in. Perennials in mulched beds usually need watering only in exceptionally dry conditions, when they will need the same attention from sprinklers and hoses as your other garden plants.

In late summer and early autumn it is usually necessary to cut back dead flowers and dying stems and leaves from some of your more unsightly perennials. You can tidy up beds and borders at the same time, hoeing out any weeds.

A bonus with some early flowering perennials, such as lupins and delphiniums, is that they will flower again in later summer if they are dead-headed as soon as their first flowers fade.

Problem perennials

A few perennial plants do present problems, but you can find ways to avoid these. Some, for example, do much better than others and become garden thugs, swamping and overwhelming slower and gentler-growing plants. Avoid perennials such as *Archillea ptarmica* 'The Pearl' as it is a very invasive plant. To keep it under control you will have to divide it every year.

Some older varieties are prone to diseases such as rust and mildew. Michaelmas daisies, in particular, are affected by mildew, but this can be largely avoided by buying new varieties that are disease resistant. Some perennials lose their vigour after a few years and so are not such good value.

GROWING FROM SEED

Some perennials can be grown from seed but it is a lengthy and often challenging process. If you think it is worth growing from seed, you are wise to buy from a reliable seed merchant or your plants may be of uneven or poor quality. Sow indoors or under glass from mid-winter.

GROWING TIPS

Photos Horticultural

Lupins, for example, should be replaced every few years. Hollyhocks get rust spots on their leaves: this can be controlled by spraying but it may be simpler to replace with new plants.

Tall perennials need staking to prevent them flopping over in winds or after rain. Some of medium height also need staking and this can be time-consuming and a bit unsightly in the middle of an ornamental border. Avoid perennials that are too tall or choose varieties that are known to be self-supporting, such as the Belladonna hybrid group of delphiniums rather than those with very tall spikes. Try *D. belladonna* 'Blue Bees'.

Tall-growing hollyhocks (far right) are fairly sturdy but should be staked unless in a sheltered site.

Tall perennials will need staking against rain and wind damage. Whatever form of support is used it should be put in place early to avoid damaging the plants. There are several options. Ready-made frames can be bought from garden centres. A framework of twiggy pea sticks, carefully inserted in a clump to a height of 90cm/3ft, will soon be covered by foliage. Single tall spikes can be staked with a bamboo cane, but the best option for groups of flowers is to form a 'cage'. Insert three canes and circle them with wire or garden twine (right).

The epimediums form excellent ground cover. Epimedium × perralchicum (right) has evergreen heart-shaped leaves and produces yellow flowers in spring.

Photos Horticultural

Peter McHoy

Daffodils

Easy to grow, quick to multiply and available in an astonishing variety of enchanting spring flowers, the popular and colourful daffodil earns its place in the garden of any size.

Photos Horticultural

With their brilliant golden cups, daffodils are the star of the narcissus family, the most popular of all the spring-flowering bulbs. Every garden has a place for one of the many varieties, whether tall, large-cupped and stately, or small and delicately nodding.

The growing cycle
Daffodil bulbs start their growing period in the autumn and continue slowly throughout the winter months. By spring, their foliage emerges above ground, just ahead of the crowning flowers.

After flowering, daffodils form seed pods while the bulbs go into a period of replenishment, replacing nutrients. They also multiply, producing 'bulblets', which eventually develop into full-size bulbs.

In early summer the daffodil's long, narrow leaves die down and the plant takes a rest until autumn.

Sunshine colours
The flower head consists of a trumpet or cup (the *corona*), surrounded by petals (the *perianth segments*). Some varieties of daffodil have double cups – a cup within a cup – or many layers of petals.

Yellow is the most common colour, from pale to dark, but there are also white daffodils,

Narcissi or daffodils are seen at their best when growing in drifts (right) and this is a planting pattern that is often used in formal gardens (facing page). The gloriously bright yellow daffodil 'Golden Harvest' (inset) grows up to 45cm/18in tall.

Photos Horticultural

and other varieties with two separate colours – yellow and orange, white and yellow, or white and orange. Pink and white varieties are relative newcomers to the host of mainstream varieties and because of this they are more expensive to buy.

Daffodils come in various heights, from miniatures or dwarfs, just 8–15cm/4–6in tall, to the tallest varieties of regal trumpet daffodils which may reach 50cm/20in. There are masses of varieties to choose from, and these fall into the following main groupings:

Trumpet daffodils are among the most popular. Each flower has a long, prominent cup; most are yellow, but there are also many other white varieties.

Large-cupped daffodils are tall, like trumpet daffodils, growing up to 50cm/20in. Each flower has a cup-shaped centre, generally in a colour that contrasts strikingly with the petals: for instance, an orange cup surrounded by yellow petals.

Double daffodils are blooms which consist of many petals, or have a double cup, and come in a range of colours, including yellow, and combinations of yellow and white. These are also tall-growing daffodils, topping 45cm/18in.

Poeticus narcissi are valued for their very late, often sweetly scented flowers, consisting of a tiny coloured cup against white petals. These are produced on stems reaching up to 40cm/16in tall.

Triandrus narcissi are the dwarf forms, bearing clusters of drooping yellow or white flowers on stems which grow to 15–30cm/6–12in in height.

Cyclamineus narcissi are an immensely popular group

The dwarf variety 'Jumblie' (right) has delicate, 'nodding' swept-back petals. Growing to just 15–30cm/6–12in, they are less likely to topple over in fierce winds.

Photos Horticultural

There are many superb double flower varieties of narcissi now available and 'Texas' (below) is a fine example, with a glowing orange tinge to its central petals.

Sidney Moulds/The Garden Picture Library

Colourful contrasts: the white petals and creamy yellow trumpet of tall-growing 'Ice Follies' (right) serves as an excellent foil to a deeper yellow variety. 'Semper Avanti' (far right) has a classic combination of translucent white petals and vibrant gold trumpet, while tall, large-cupped 'Carlton' (below right) displays its buttery hues to the best effect in large clumps.

PLANT PROFILE

Suitable site and soil: sun or light shade; in most soils, but must be well drained.

Planting: make a hole three times the depth of the bulb.

Cultivation and care: dig in plenty of garden compost before planting. Add gravel or sand to aid drainage. After flowering, feed regularly and allow the leaves to die down.

Propagation: break off small bulblets and re-plant.

Pests and diseases: mainly trouble-free, but liable to rot in badly-drained soil.

Recommended varieties:
Tall:
Yellow
'Carlton' (large cupped)
'Dutch Master' (trumpet)
'Golden Ducat' (double)

'Golden Harvest' (trumpet)
'King Alfred' (trumpet)
'Magnificence' (trumpet)
'Unsurpassable' (trumpet)
Yellow and orange
'Fortune' (large cupped)
'Scarlet O'Hara' (large cupped)
'Texas' (double)
White
'Cheerfulness' (double)
'Mount Hood' (trumpet)
'White Lion' (double)
White and yellow
'Actaea' (poeticus)
'Flower Record' (large cupped)
'Old Pheasant Eye' (poeticus)
'Semper Avanti' (large cupped)

Miniature or dwarf:
Yellow
'February Gold' (cyclamineus)

'Jumblie' (cyclamineus)
'Liberty Bells' (triandrus)
Narcissus bulbocodium (wild)
Narcissus cyclamineus (wild)
'Peeping Tom' (cyclamineus)
'Tête-à-tête' (cyclamineus)
Yellow and orange
'March Sunshine' (cyclamineus)
'Suzy' (jonquil)
White
'February Silver' (cyclamineus)
'Jenny' (cyclamineus)
Narcissus triandrus albus (wild)
'Silver Chimes' (triandrus)
'Thalia' (triandrus)
White and yellow
'Jack Snipe' (cyclamineus)
'Dove Wings' (cyclamineus)
'Little Beauty' (trumpet)

that consist mainly of dwarf varieties (15–30cm/6–12in) derived from the wild species, *Narcissus cyclamineus*. These boast the highly distinctive flowers of the species: long trumpets and swept-back petals, which give the impression that they are facing into a strong wind. The flowers are yellow or white or bi-coloured. **Jonquils** have sweetly fragrant clusters of yellow or white flowers and grow up to 15–30cm/6–12in high.

Buying bulbs

Garden centres offer a good range of varieties, but if you want a wider choice buy from a specialist bulb grower. They sell by mail order and supply

John Glover

well-illustrated catalogues.

For the maximum number of flowers buy the largest bulbs available of that particular species and variety. Choose your bulbs as soon as they appear in the shops; if left for too long on the shelves they will deteriorate. Avoid any with blemishes, loose outer skins or softness around the base where the roots will show. This usually means the bulbs have been displayed in conditions that are too warm.

Getting the best effect

The taller-growing daffodils make excellent cut flowers so, if you have enough space, rather than spoil your main garden display, grow a row specially for cutting. They will

grow virtually anywhere, so you need not worry about providing exactly the right sort of conditions. They do thrive, however, in sun or light shade.

For the best effect daffodils should be planted boldly in drifts or groups of irregular shape. The miniature and dwarf varieties look particularly effective in rock gardens, between paving stones or at the front of mixed borders.

The taller-growing daffodils look best planted near shrubs, particularly spring-flowering kinds such as deutzia, forsythia, flowering currant (ribes), magnolias and camellias.

Natural attraction

Daffodils look very attractive growing in lawns, especially in

Gillian Beckett

Andrew Lawson

clumps under a tree. You can use any type, but especially recommended are the poeticus, trumpet and large-cupped varieties.

You can use daffodils for spring bedding but, in this case, you must lift the bulbs after flowering and replant them elsewhere to make way for summer bedding plants.

Trumpet, large-cupped and double daffodils are best for spring bedding. Grow them in bold groups with blue forget-me-nots and polyanthus.

Preparing the site

Daffodils will grow in a wide range of soils but the site must be well drained, as the bulbs are liable to rot if the soil is wet or waterlogged over the winter months.

Dig the ground thoroughly before planting, adding very well-rotted manure or garden compost. If the drainage is poor then mix plenty of coarse

Collections/Patrick Johns

PROJECT PLANTING IN GRASS

Photos Horticultural

To plant narcissus bulbs in a lawn or rough grass, scatter them gently in the area. This creates a more natural look, as you can plant the bulbs almost where they land. Using a bulb planter, make a hole for the bulb to almost three times its depth. If the bulb is planted in more shallow soil, it is less likely to flower well and naturalize – produce new bulblets. Put a little sand in the base of the hole and set the bulb in firmly, making sure there are no air pockets beneath. Add some peat and a sprinkling of bone meal to give the bulb a good start, then return the soil to the hole. Press down firmly and water the area well.

Tiny Narcissus bulbocodium (left), a wild variety, looks especially attractive in a rock garden. The little cup fans out from the delicately spiked petals, rather like a hooped petticoat. Growing to a neat 8-15cm/3-6in, this slender-leafed species naturalizes vigorously if planted in moist soil in a sunny site.

PERFECT PARTNERS

Create striking spring bedding arrangements by using creamy pale narcissi to offset vivid-coloured, low growing perennials. Here, Narcissus poeticus 'Actaea' harmonizes with the vibrant blue and yellow of polyanthus 'Crescendo Blue'.

Tania Midgley

'Jack Snipe' (below) a small white and yellow Cyclamineus narcissus, is one that naturalizes well in small corners. A sturdy variety, which grows to 23cm/9in, it flowers in early to mid-spring. The creamy white petals are distinctively swept back from its narrow, lemon-coloured cup.

Tania Midgley

sand or grit into the soil.

At planting time, apply a sprinkling of bone meal mixed with peat, which releases food to the bulbs slowly over the winter.

Buy the bulbs when you are ready to plant them, ideally in late summer or early autumn. When planting in informal groups or drifts, scatter the bulbs on the ground first and then plant them where they fall (within reason). This gives a natural, clumped look. Space large daffodils 10–20cm/4–8in apart and dwarf and miniature varieties about 8cm/3in apart.

The depth of the planting varies according to the size of the bulb. The largest bulbs should be set into 15cm/6in deep holes, the smallest into 8cm/3in holes.

Planting tips

Dig your bulb holes with a hand trowel or with a special bulb planter. This neat gadget takes out a core of soil, then replaces it when the bulb has been set in the hole. It is essential that each bulb sits firmly at the bottom of the hole because if there is a gap the bulb may fail to root and grow.

After planting, water the area thoroughly, especially if the soil is dry. Bulbs will not start growing in dry conditions.

For the future . . .

Remove dead flowerheads to prevent the plant setting seed. After flowering, feed the soil around the remaining foliage with a general-purpose liquid fertilizer. This ensures a good flower display the following year. Give two or three feeds at weekly or fortnightly intervals, first making sure the soil is moist so that the fertilizer is absorbed efficiently.

Allow the leaves to die down completely before cutting them back as they replace all the nutrients taken out of the bulbs with flowering. If grown in grass, do not mow the area of lawn around the bulbs until the foliage has withered, nor tie the leaves together.

Forget-me-nots

The azure blue forget-me-not, native to stream edges and meadows, has also been a garden favourite for centuries. Today it comes in a wide range of flower tones.

The forget-me-not family includes four of the most charming and easily grown flowers the amateur gardener could wish for – all in enchanting shades of blue. Whatever the soil type or location of your garden there will be a forget-me-not that will be only too happy to grow there.

Although you may not be familiar with its Latin name, you will recognise myosotis, the garden forget-me-not, a familiar partner to the spring bulbs and wallflowers. In fact, there are several other lesser known plants in the forget-me-not family, and they are every bit as deserving of a place in your garden.

Shades of blue

The other main plants in the family are omphalodes, lithospermum and anchusa. Despite their different names, these plants are botanically related. From the gardener's point of view, what unites them is that they all have blue flowers, in every conceivable shade, from pale powder blue to sky blue, ultramarine, gentian and even violet. Often the blue is enhanced by a white or yellow 'eye' in the centre of the bloom. Sometimes pink shades occur along with the blue – some open from pink buds, others have pink streaks or turn pink as they develop. Although the flowers are quite small, they are freely produced, often for long periods.

Cottage charm

Forget-me-nots have everything to recommend them. Blue is often a hard colour to get into the garden – pink and yellow shades abound, but blue is much less common. Forget-me-nots are hardy plants, they are easy to grow, and, because they self-seed easily, most will keep coming back year after year with very little attention from you. The only virtue that most lack is

Eric Crichton

Harry Smith Collection

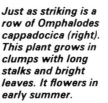

A fine display for rock gardens is created by the Myosotis alpestris 'Blue Ball' (left). Its fragrant flowers bloom from late spring.

Just as striking is a row of Omphalodes cappadocica (right). This plant grows in clumps with long stalks and bright leaves. It flowers in early summer.

Tania Midgley

The rich, deep colour of this Anchusa azurea, 'Loddon Royalist' (left), shows why it is among the most popular of forget-me-nots. It grows as high as 1m/3ft and blends excitingly with other strong tones when the flowers bloom through the summer.

The more subtle shades of the Lithospermum oleifolium (below left) are ideally suited to rock gardens. A hardy plant, it produces pink buds which flower from late spring onwards and spreads freely. It can also be grown successfully with alpines.

A basket makes an unusual container for forget-me-nots and painted it brings out the colour of the flowers.
When using a basket (below, right) line it first with thick plastic. Be sure to remember to make holes in the sheeting. Then almost fill with compost.

PLANT PROFILE

MYOSOTIS

Myosotis sylvatica is a hardy biennial with white- or yellow-centred, soft blue, pink or white flowers. Spring flowering, it is ideal for planting under bulbs or with wallflowers. *Myosotis alpestris* and *Myosotis rupicola* are small perennials which grow well in the rock garden.
Suitable site and soil: shade and moist soil are recommended, but the plants are so hardy they flourish almost anywhere.
Cultivation and care: sow seed outdoors in late spring to flower the following year.
Propagation: the plants self-seed freely – allow them to spread at will, or collect the ripe seed and scatter it where required.
Pests and diseases: uncommon.

OMPHALODES

This hardy semi-evergreen perennial forms large clumps or mats. Use on rockeries or as ground cover. Its blue flowers are larger than those of *myosotis*.
Suitable site and soil: does best in partial shade and moist peaty soil.
Cultivation and care: buy plants in mid-spring. Water plentifully in hot weather.
Propagation: divide and replant in midsummer, or sow seeds in a cold frame and pot up singly.
Pests and diseases: uncommon.

LITHOSPERMUM

Use this mat-forming hardy evergreen perennial on rockeries, to trail from the tops of open stone walls, or as ground cover. Its funnel-shaped blue flowers are shaded with pink.
Suitable site and soil: loves full sun in well-drained soil. *L. diffusum* dislikes lime.
Cultivation and care: set out in mid-spring, enriching soil with peat or leaf-mould.
Propagation: take cuttings from soft lateral shoots in mid- to late summer.
Pests and diseases: uncommon.

ANCHUSA

There is a tall hardy perennial for herbaceous borders and a small hardy annual for bedding and containers. The perennials have blue flowers, the annuals are also available in mixtures of blue shades, pink and white.
Suitable site and soil: sunny spot in any good garden soil.
Cultivation: for annuals, sow seed in spring, or buy plants. For perennials, plant between mid-autumn and early spring. Support with twiggy sticks and cut down by half after flowering to encourage a second show. Cut down old stems in mid-autumn.
Propagation: take root cuttings of perennials in winter; plant in a cold frame. Transfer to a nursery bed in spring, plant out during the following autumn.
Pests and diseases: uncommon.

scent. By using different members of the family, you can spread their beautiful blues across your borders, rockery, containers, walls, wild areas and even the garden pond for much of the year.

The common garden forget-me-not is *Myosotis sylvatica* (sometimes wrongly listed as *Myosotis alpestris*). Its clouds of dainty, pale blue flowers with a white or yellow eye used to be seen in every cottage garden, appearing in mid-spring and continuing into summer. Nowadays there are

Harry Smith Collection

Insight Picture Library

Pat Brindley

also varieties with deep blue, pink or white flowers. Some, such as 'Royal Blue', 'True Blue' and 'Bouquet', grow 23-30cm/9-12in high and are suitable for borders or for cutting. Others, such as 'Blue Ball', 'Carmine King' and 'Miniature Blue', are shorter (about 15cm/6in high) and more compact. All have spear-shaped, bright green, slightly hairy leaves.

Myosotis is actually a hardy biennial, but it is so free-seeding that it can be treated more like a perennial. *Myosotis alpestris* is the proper name of the alpine or perennial forget-me-not. This is a sturdier plant, growing about 20cm/8in high; the flowers have a pronounced yellow eye. *Myosotis rupicola* is only 7.5cm/3in high.

Shady customer

Omphalodes is a small, neat, hardy perennial, only 10-23cm/4-9in high, ideal for rockeries or for use as ground cover. Its common name is navelwort – a name almost as unattractive as its Latin one – and it has similar but much larger flowers than myosotis. The leaves are long-stemmed, heart-shaped and smooth, forming a thick carpet up to 60cm/2ft across. In mild areas the plant is evergreen, and it grows best in cool, moist shade.

Omphalodes cappadocica is the biggest, showiest species, bearing plentiful sprays of

The water forget-me-not, Myosotis palustris, adds a new shade to a tranquil scene (above).

The 'Heavenly Blue' variety of Lithospermum diffusum has a delightful, sprawling look (below) which makes it an ideal choice for under-planting a small tree.

Tania Midgley

sky-blue flowers with white centres in early to midsummer. *Omphalodes verna* (also known as blue-eyed Mary) is valuable for winter colour, as the bright blue, white-centred flowers appear from late winter through to late spring. A white-flowered variety is also available. Avoid *Omphalodes luciliae*, which is a more fussy plant and less showy.

Superb ground cover

A mat-forming hardy perennial, the evergreen lithospermum makes excellent ground cover. It can also be grown in the rock garden, or planted to hang down from the top of an open stone wall.

The best species to have is *Lithospermum diffusum*. It

Forget-me-not Anchusa azurea 'Loddon Royalist' (below) has a shade described as gentian-blue. Though less forceful than the tone of the 'Royal Blue' variety, its colour is captivating. These tall plants enjoy space and should be planted at least 30cm/12in apart. They self-seed easily.

Andrew Lawson

grows no more than 10cm/4in high, but spreads for as much as 60cm/2ft. The flowers are funnel shaped and an intense gentian blue colour, with a basal tube tinged with reddish-violet stripes giving an interesting two-tone effect to the display. The carpet of narrow, deep green leaves makes the plant attractive all year round, and the flowers appear for a long period, from early summer to mid-autumn. Two popular varieties are 'Grace Ward', with large, intense blue flowers, and 'Heavenly Blue', with flowers of an even deeper, richer blue.

Fitting soils

The only snag with this useful plant is that it needs lime-free soil. If your soil is limey, then look for *Lithospermum oleifolium*. This is taller and less spreading, with grey-green leaves and sky-blue flowers that open from pink buds. Another possibility is *Lithospermum purpureo-caeruleum*, which is taller – up to 30cm/1ft high – with violet-blue, almost purple, flowers. This grows happily in the driest of chalky soils.

Although a member of the forget-me-not family, anchusa is commonly known as alkanet or bugloss. The species includes two very different plants – a large perennial suitable for growing in borders, and a hardy annual very popular for summer bedding. There is also an alpine, *Anchusa caespitosa* (tufted alkanet) but this needs to be grown with alpines or in a scree bed.

Appeal to bees

The annual *Anchusa capensis* is the most similar to the garden forget-me-not, as it is small (about 23cm/9in high) and compact, with masses of white- or yellow-centred flowers from early summer to early autumn. Two very popular varieties are 'Blue Angel', with intense ultramarine blue flowers, and 'Dawn', a mixture containing lavender, pink and white flowers as well as blue ones. Both are very attractive to bees.

Anchusa italica or *A. azurea* is 90cm-1.7m/3-5ft high. Although it does not live long, it self-seeds freely. The saucer-shaped blue flowers are tiny, but produced in great profusion from early to late summer. They grow in upright spikes distracting attention from the coarse foliage.

PERFECT PARTNERS

You can create some stunning effects by mixing forget-me-nots with other brightly-coloured complementary flowers. This daring blend (right) of forget-me-nots and tulips is enhanced by the addition of a few wallflowers.

Always plant the annuals or biennials before the tulip bulbs, so that you can see where they are, and use the taller types of forget-me-not. This will provide just the right contrast in heights. Use the mid-seasonal or late varieties of tulip so that they bloom in late spring at the same time as the forget-me-nots. With such rich colours, keep to two or three tones to avoid a fussy look which distracts from the overall impression.

Peter McHoy

Stately Hyacinths

Sweet-smelling hyacinths bring spring colour to the garden and can banish the drabness of winter from normally flowerless rooms.

Of all the spring bulbs, hyacinths are perhaps the most widely used for indoor cultivation, providing bold colour and a sweet, pervasive fragrance from Christmas to Easter when grown indoors in bowls or pots. But these versatile performers can also give fine displays in outdoor beds or in window-boxes and tubs through the spring. Indeed, they may start their lives as indoor plants, perhaps as Christmas gifts, and go on to give many years of pleasure in the garden.

For most people, the image of the hyacinth that will most immediately spring to mind is that of the tubular-flowered hybrids commonly known as Dutch hyacinths, varieties of *Hyacinthus orientalis*. This large bulb produces a single, heavily-scented flower spike 10-15cm/4-6in long. This spike is tightly packed with small, bell-shaped flowers.

Varieties of Dutch hyacinth can be purchased in a wide range of clear colours: its blooms may be white, cream, yellow, pink, red or blue. New varieties and shades appear every year.

Left to their own devices in the garden, Dutch hyacinths will flower from mid to late spring, although they can be persuaded to flower earlier indoors by a technique known as 'forcing'. Special, treated bulbs which can be forced into flower by Christmas are also widely

Hyacinths are famed for their sweet scent and vivid colour, especially shades of blue. H. 'Ostara' (right) verges on indigo.

Tania Midgley

Pat Brindley

PLANT PROFILE

Suitable site and soil Both Dutch hyacinths and grape hyacinths will grow in full sun or light shade, in well-drained soil.

Planting Plant Dutch hyacinths 15cm/6in deep in early to mid autumn. Grape hyacinths should be planted at the same time, but at half the depth.

Cutlivation and care They need little care during the growing season except for water in dry spells. After flowering, remove dead blooms but leave the stalk intact. Leaves and flower stems should be left to wither and die naturally.

Propagation Prepare Dutch hyacinths by slitting the base of the bulb two or three times with a sharp knife in the autumn before planting. This encourages the growth of small offsets which may later be separated and planted out. Prepared bulbs cannot be propagated.

Grape hyacinths seed themselves rapidly: alternatively, lift and divide them every three years when the foliage has yellowed.

Pests and diseases Stem and bulb eelworm causes pale stripes on leaves, followed by twisted growth and deformed flowers and leaves. Infested bulbs are soft and may have a white woolly substance on the base. Healthy bulbs from reputable sources are usually sterilized against eelworm. Infested bulbs must be dug up and destroyed. Soft rot bacteria can occasionally attack pot-grown hyacinths. Flowers fail to develop and topple over at soil level while still in bud. This is precipitated by moist, humid conditions. Beware of over-watering.

Hyacinths are usually sold and planted in single colours. If you want a multi-coloured display in flower at the same time, buy a collection such as 'Multiflora Mixed' (above).

The Roman hyacinth (H. orientalis albulus) is smaller than the species but produces two or three headily fragrant, loosely packed, flower spikes. 'Rosalie' (right) is a good pink variety; others are blue or white. Dutch hyacinths such as the rich pink 'Jan Bos' (below) have a single, more compact spike.

Eric Crichton

Harry Smith Collection

available in garden centres.

A smaller subspecies, the Roman hyacinth (*H. orientalis albulus*) produces two or three flower spikes 15cm/6in high. These are thinner than those of the species, with fewer, more widely-spaced and stronger-scented white, pink or blue flowers. Like all hyacinths, it is frost hardy, but it does best when grown indoors and is the easiest of the varieties to force.

Outdoors, it will flower slightly earlier than the Dutch hyacinth; indoors, any time

GARDEN NOTES

CHRISTMAS BLOOMS

If you want your bulbs to be in flower for Christmas it is essential to buy specially prepared bulbs. These are widely available in garden centres from late summer and the same instructions apply as for untreated bulbs, but the pots should be brought in when shoots are 2.5cm/1in high, not later than the beginning of winter.

Gillain Beckett

RECOMMENDED VARIETIES

Dutch Hyacinth All share the same characteristics of size and shape and differ mainly by their colour. There are several in differing shades of pink, ranging from the pale pink 'Lady Derby', and the slightly darker 'Pink Pearl' to the crimson 'Jan Bos'. 'L'Innocence' is a creamy white and 'City of Haarlem' a pale yellow. At the other end of the spectrum come the delicate pale blues of 'Bismark' and 'Delft Blue', and the striking indigo 'Ostara'.

Grape Hyacinths Most commonly available are *Muscari azureum* (also known as *Hyacinthus azureus*), which has clear blue flowers, darker towards the base of the spike, and *Muscari armenaicum*, which has pale blue flowers tipped with white. It can often also be found in the white form 'Album'. Both grow to a height of about 20cm/8in.

Muscari latifolium is sometimes seen. This is slightly larger (25cm/10in), and its long, two-tone flower is a deep blackish-violet, topped by a smaller layer of bright blue petals. The rather odd-looking tassel or feather hyacinth (*Muscari comosum*), as its name suggests, looks something like a feather duster. It is most often available in a form known as 'Plumosum' or 'Monstrosum', which has light, pinkish-blue flowers and grows to around 30cm/12in.

from midwinter to early spring.

The very large-bulbed Multiflora hyacinth produces nine to twelve 15cm/6in flower stalks per bulb, with blooms in shades of white, pink or blue. Like the Roman hyacinth, it does best indoors, where it has the same flowering season.

Grape hyacinths

The smaller plants known as grape hyacinths belong to a different, but closely related genus of bulb, *Muscari*. However, with their tightly-packed flower spikes, they are suffi- ciently reminiscent of their larger cousin to merit their common name. In most species the petals of the individual flowers curve in, rather than out, giving them narrow mouths. Colours range from white through various shades of blue to a deep bluish purple which is almost black; only some species are fragrant.

Fast growers

Grape hyacinths are easy to grow and look their best in groups at the front of borders or as edging to mixed beds. They are also ideal rock garden plants and do well in tubs and window-boxes. The many different varieties can be seen in flower any time from early spring to midsummer.

Their only drawback is the speed with which they proliferate, especially *Muscari racemosum* syn. *Muscari neglectum*, which is really only suitable for wilder parts of the

Andrew Lawson

Planting mixed colour schemes (right) can be problematical because different varieties can flower a few days, even weeks apart. Here, 'Delft Blue' is fully mature, while the white spikes of 'L'Innocence' have yet to emerge completely from the green.

As with most other Dutch hyacinths, the leaves of 'Pink Pearl' (left) do not develop fully until after the plant has flowered.

'City of Haarlem' (left) has a distinct, pale yellow tint.

Varieties of the grape hyacinth Muscari armenaicum such as 'Blue Spike' (right) have a distinctive white fringe around the flower openings.

Pat Brindley

Pat Brindley

garden. With other species, divide and replant bulbs every three years after the leaves have turned yellow at the end of the growing season.

Rocky origins

The species form of *Hyacinthus orientalis*, which resembles the modern Roman hyacinth, is a native of western Asia, where it can be found growing amongst the rocks. The numerous wild varieties of grape hyacinths are also found in scrubby, rocky areas of western Asia and the eas-

GROWING TIPS

RECYCLING HOUSE PLANTS

After a forced hyacinth has flowered, remove the dead heads by running a hand up the stem from the base of the flower spike. Do not cut off the stalk. Continue watering until the leaves have withered and died down, then allow the compost to dry out, remove the bulbs and, having picked off any dried compost, dead roots or foliage, store in a cool, dry place until the autumn, when they may be planted out in the garden, with a little slow-acting fertilizer, such as bone meal, worked into the soil.

Bulbs grown in compost will often flower outdoors during their first spring, but those grown in bulb fibre will need more time to recover. Neither can be brought in and used again as houseplants.

FORCING

Hyacinths can be made to flower indoors from midwinter. Bulbs for forcing should be potted up at the end of the summer. They can be planted singly in 10-12cm/4-5in pots but look best when planted together in larger pots or bowls. Whatever you choose, make sure the bulb has room to develop roots. It is not a good idea to mix colours in containers as it is difficult to bring all of the colours into flower together.

In pots without drainage holes, a special bulb fibre should be used. For those with drainage holes, use a good potting compost – John Innes No. 1 or No. 2 would be fine.

Place a layer of moist compost or very moist (but not sodden) bulb fibre at the bottom of the container and set the bulbs on it, close together but not touching. Press them down very gently so that their bases are in firm contact with the compost. Making sure that they remain steadily upright, continue adding compost until the tops of the bulbs are just showing.

They now need about six to ten weeks of complete darkness in a temperature of not more than 5°C/40°F. Commercial growers bury them under peat until they are rooted and it is quite possible to do this at home, but it is just as effective to place the container in a black polythene bag and stand it in a cool corner of the garden. Check the bulbs occasionally to ensure the compost is still moist, but take care not to over-water.

When the shoot tips are around 2.5-5cm/1-2in high, bring the bowl indoors into a cool place (not more than 10°C/50°F), gradually increasing the amount of light and raising the temperature as more shoots appear.

As the leaves develop and flower buds appear, move the container to a bright, draught-free site around 15-20°C/60-70°F. Keep the compost moist at all times and turn the bowl occasionally to make sure you get even growth.

Far and away the most unusual plant in the hyacinth group is the tassel grape hyacinth (Muscari comosum 'Plumosum' syn. 'Monstrosum'), whose sterile flowers are superseded by a mass of purple threads (above). More conventionally shaped, but a startlingly clear white, is M. azureum album (left). The most vigorous member of the genus, though, is the deep blue M. neglectum syn. M. racemosum (right), which self-seeds rapidly and will soon take over a formal planting; it is best used in a semi-wild setting.

PERFECT PARTNERS

Hyacinths do not always suit companion planting. However, H. 'L'Innocence' is at home among the pink blooms of the low-growing double daisy Bellis perennis 'Rose Carpet'.

tern Mediterranean.

Given their origins, it is not surprising that both will flourish best in open, sunny situations with well-drained soil, although both will also tolerate partial shade, which will in fact extend their flowering period for a month or so.

Buying hyacinths

Dutch hyacinth bulbs are usually sold by size. For outdoor planting it is advisable to buy the smaller sized bulbs (16-17cm in circumference). The flower heads may not be as big, but they will be better able to withstand the squally weather of early spring.

For outside flowering, both hyacinth and grape hyacinth bulbs should be planted in early or mid autumn. Both look their best planted in small clumps rather than standing in rows like well-drilled soldiers, and both blend very well with daffodils.

Hyacinths should be planted to a depth of 15cm/6in and spaced 15-20cm/6-8in apart, and grape hyacinths to a depth of 8cm/3in, 10cm/4in apart. Some well-rotted compost or peat dug into the site a few days before planting will get your bulbs off to a good start.

HYACINTH JARS

Single hyacinths are often grown in glass bulb jars, which are sold in most gardening shops. The jar should be filled with water to a point just below the base of the bulb (*not* touching it). A small piece of charcoal in the bottom of the jar will help to keep the water fresh.

The jar should be kept in a cool, dark place until the roots are about 10cm/4in long and the leaves have begun to show, when it should be moved into a warmer and lighter spot.

Make sure the jar is kept topped up with water to the required level. Water-grown bulbs should be discarded at the end of their growing season as they will not flower again.

Versatile Irises

Versatile and easy to grow, irises make an elegant addition to the flower garden. Plant them around the pond, in borders or in rockeries for year round colour.

Irises form a very large genus of flowering perennials with more than 300 members, most of them ideally suited to gardens. There is, quite literally, an iris for every situation, from a pond, through moist boggy areas to a dry sun-parched border.

By choosing the right varieties you can have irises blooming in every season, their flowers ranging from the purest white, through sunny yellows to the deepest, velvety purple. With some varieties there is the added bonus of a delicious scent, and nearly all types make good cut flowers.

A typical iris is easily recognized by its erect, sword-shaped leaves and distinctive flowers, made up of three inner petals (standards) which usually stand upright, and three larger, outer ones (falls) which fall downwards.

Iris groups

For convenience, commonly-grown garden irises can be split into three main groups, each serving a different purposes in the garden. Bulbous irises include the various border kinds, popular as florists' cut flowers, as well as dwarf, winter and spring alpine species. Water irises grow best in moist soil or shallow water and are ideal for ponds and pools. Bearded irises – so-called because of a line of fleshy hairs on the falls which looks like a beard – are traditionally grown in the herbaceous border and include the

Bearded irises (left and facing page) are so named because of the hairs on the petals.

popular 'flag' irises.

The most popular hybrids found in garden centres and bulb catalogues are known as English, Dutch and Spanish irises. English irises derive from *I. latifolia*, Spanish from *I. xiphium*, while the Dutch are hybrids. They have similar, wide ranges of colour.

Given a sunny position in the garden, they are as trouble-free as any of the common spring bulbs, and should be planted in the autumn for a succession of flowers throughout the summer months.

Continuous flowers

The Dutch are the first to flower, in early summer, followed in a few weeks by the Spanish and then by the English. By planting a few bulbs of each type, it is possible to have a continuous supply of white, yellow, blue, mauve and purple flowers for cutting, or simply for enjoying in the garden border. The plants will grow to a height of 30-60cm/12-24in.

The Dutch and Spanish irises may not be hardy in some colder areas, and will need

In late winter, I. reticulata (right) can bring vibrant colour to a rockery or window box.

The delightful water iris, I. laevigata alba (above right), flowers in midsummer.

I. laevigata (far right), flanked by Euphorbia griffithii 'Fireglow', can make a striking display.

The tiny I. danfordiae (below), with glowing yellow flowers, is perfect for a rockery.

Andrew Lawson

Eric Crichton

protecting in winter with a cloche. The English irises are the easiest of all to grow, needing no winter protection.

Equally pretty are the dwarf irises, which flower in early spring. They prefer a well-drained soil and make ideal specimens for rockeries and alpine beds, or for growing in pots on the patio; they also make a brave show in a winter window box, where their bright colours are especially welcome in late winter.

I. reticulata grows to just 15cm/6in in height, and produces a delicate, sweetly-scented, blue or purple flower, while *I. danfordiae* is strongly scented and even smaller, just 5-10cm/2-4in tall. The yellow flowers have green spots on the fall petals, while the standards are under-developed; the flowers are rarely as much as 5cm/2in across.

Water lovers

Water irises grow from rhizomes, or fleshy roots, and are best suited to waterside planting. Two species, *Iris kaempferi* and *Iris laevigata*, have beautiful, big flowers, 12-15cm/5-6in across. *I. kaempferi* is happiest in moist soil on

Harry Smith Collection

Clive Nicholas/Garden Picture Library

GARDEN NOTES

DIVIDE AND RULE

You can increase your stock of irises by dividing up clumps which have become overgrown.

Lift bulbous irises when the foliage has died down (usually in late summer). The bulbs will spilt naturally by hand and once replanted will often flower the following year.

Rhizomes can be divided in the same way. Lift them after flowering, then, using a sharp knife, cut off new pieces from the outside and discard the old centre. Each piece should have one or two strong offshoots. Replant immediately.

Eric Crichton

Eric Crichton

the edge of the pool, while *I. laevigata* is a true water plant, and ideally likes 15cm/6in of water above the rhizome. Both varieties flower in early to midsummer.

Many water irises originate in Japan – indeed the group is sometimes known as Japanese irises – but *I. sibirica* comes from Siberia. It prefers boggy soil, and grows to 1.2m/4ft, with blue or purple flowers in early summer. Its hybrids, in blue, violet and white, are good garden choices.

The yellow flag iris (*Iris pseudacorus*), with its butter-coloured flowers, grows wild in Britain and is very adaptable, accustoming itself to any water depth up to 46cm/18in. It can reach 1.8m/6ft tall.

Water irises are completely hardy and need no special care. If they start to outgrow the pond, the rhizomes can easily be divided and replanted every three years or so.

Border favourites

The bearded irises also grow from rhizomes, but they are distinguised by a 'beard' of hairs on the downward petals. This group, mainly derived from *I. pallida* and *I. germanica*, contains most of the com-

RECOMMENDED VARIETIES

Dwarf bulbs
I. reticulata 'Harmony'; velvet blue with yellow blaze. 'Violet Beauty'; purple with orange streak.
I. danfordiae; yellow.

Other bulbs
'White Excelsior'; white Dutch. 'Imperator'; deep blue. 'Golden Emperor'; gold.

Water irises
I. kaempferi; purple, pink, lavender or white marginal or bog plant.
Yellow flag (*I. pseudacorus*); yellow water plant.
I. laevigata; blue or purple marginal. 'Snowdrift' is a pure white double, 'Regal' is red. 'Variegata' has blue flowers and leaves striped with white.

Bearded irises
Purple flag (*I. germanica*); medium-sized rich purple with white beard.
I. pallida 'Bold Print'; medium, white and purple. 'Early Light'; tall, cream and yellow. 'Marhaba'; dwarf blue. 'Mary Frances'; tall, pink to lavender. 'Sable'; tall, with purple petals verging on black. 'Shepherd's Delight'; tall, pale pink.

J. Bain/NHPA

Neil Holmes

for the front of the border, where they will form colourful clumps through into the beginning of summer.

The tall ones flower slightly later, and are best grown at the back of the border, where other plants will give them some support. As well as the usual blue, purple and yellow, the colour range includes the pale pink of 'Shepherd's Delight', the lavender of 'Mary Frances' and the unusual golden brown, russet and white shades of 'Flamenco'.

Plant choice

The sheer number of iris varieties can make choosing the right plants for your garden a confusing task. It is really a case of deciding exactly where in the garden you want to grow them and then checking that the conditions are right for each group – moist soil or water for the Japanese irises, a sunny border for bearded and bulbous irises and a rock garden for *Iris reticulata* and the dwarf forms. Having got that right, it is simply a matter of choosing your favourite colours and getting going on the planting.

Iris reticulata bulbs should be planted 8cm/3in deep in a well-drained soil during late summer and early autumn. English, Spanish and Dutch iris bulbs should also be

mon garden hybrids. They are excellent plants for the late spring and early summer herbaceous border, as long as they have plenty of sun. Heights vary from the tiniest dwarf varieties, measuring only 10cm/4in, to the majestic tall forms which reach heights of up to 1.5m/5ft.

The spring-flowering dwarf irises, including the deep blue 'Marhaba', are best suited to rockeries where the drainage is good, while the medium-sized ones, such as 'Bold Print', whose white petals are edged with purple, are ideal

planted at this time, at a depth of 10-15cm/4-6in.

Water irises can be planted in either spring or autumn on the margins of the pond, while the rhizomes of bearded irises can be planted at the beginning or end of the summer.

The top of the rhizome should be just visible above the surface of the soil and it is important to keep them moist for the first few weeks after planting has been done.

Once established, all irises are easy to care for. They do not need attention or special watering or feeding. However, the taller varieties will benefit from staking with a bamboo cane during their first year of growth. If, after three or four years, the clumps have outgrown their allotted space, or if the flowers are poor, it is a simple task to divide them up to create new plants.

Lilies for Borders and Pots

Despite their exotic appearance, many lilies are perfectly hardy plants that will reward a little care with a long-lasting, spectacular display of flowers.

Lilies are among the most aristocratic of all garden plants, bearing their large, strikingly shaped flowers aloft on a single tall and stately stem. The flowers are often graced with exotic spots and stripes, and there are varieties in every colour bar blue.

Because lilies are so remarkably beautiful, they are considered difficult to grow, and they do generally need a little more care than more commonplace plants. But the lily family is a vast one, and far from all of its members are overly demanding. Over the last 50 years lily breeders have produced many new hybrids which are hardier and more disease-resistant than the parents, and possessed of even more magnificent flowers.

Magnificent obsession

Growing lilies is so fascinating that many gardeners become addicted, studying catalogues avidly each spring and autumn and gradually amassing large collections, featuring every lily that will flourish in their particular garden.

Although some lilies can grow very tall – the leopard lily (*Lilium pardalinum*) can exceed 2.4m/8ft – the single erect stems do not take up a lot of elbow room, so they are well suited to small gardens where they can be studied at close quarters in all their splendour. Many varieties also look well in a patio tub.

Many people are put off buying lilies because the bulbs are relatively expensive – several pounds for a single bulb in some cases. But for a small

Marijke Heuff/Garden Picture Library

Gillian Beckett

PLANT PROFILE

Suitable site and soil
Sheltered but well-ventilated spot, usually sunny, though some prefer shade. Roots must always be in shade. Rich well-drained soil – most lilies prefer acid or neutral soil, but a few tolerate or even prefer lime.

Planting Plant in spring or autumn, as soon as possible after purchase to reduce risk of drying out. If bulbs look shrivelled, keep in moist peat for 10 days first. Work coarse grit or sand into the soil to improve drainage, if necessary. Set bulb so that tip is 2½ times its height below soil level – about 7.5cm/3in for small bulbs, 10-20cm/4-8in for larger ones. Set stem-rooting lilies more deeply, and *L. candidum* and *L. × testacum*

with the tips almost showing. Plant about 23cm/9in apart, depending on ultimate height. Mark planting spot with a stick.

Cultivation and care Mulch after planting and replace regularly. Protect newly planted lilies from frost with a covering of peat. Water in dry weather, avoiding leaves. Tall plants may need staking. Cut off the flower spike when the blooms have withered.

Propagation Divide mature plants in autumn every 3-4 years, or plant bulblets or bulbils if produced.

Pests and diseases Prone to attack by a large number of pests, fungi and viruses, but spraying at the first sign of trouble will control most of them. Use wildlife-safe pellets to deter slugs.

There is plenty of choice in lily species. L. hansonii (left) has pendent orange blooms. The white petals of L. auratum (above) are up to 18cm/7in long, while the turk's caps of L. martagon (below) are smaller. The white Madonna lily (L. candidum), yellow L. 'Citronella' and orange lily make a vibrant group (right).

DON'T FORGET!

VIRUS DISEASES

Lilies are unfortunately prone to virus disease such as lily mosaic. If possible, buy guaranteed virus-free bulbs. In the growing season, keep a sharp look out for aphids, as they spread the disease. Spray at the very first sign of them.

Insight Picture Library

Gillian Beckett

garden, where quality should take precedence over quantity, the expense is more than justified by the results. Besides, once they are established, most lilies will spread, and after a few years they can very easily be divided up to produce several new plants.

A historic plant

Lilies have been cultivated for literally thousands of years. One of the best known, the pure white Madonna lily (*Lilium candidum*), was almost certainly brought to Britain by the Romans, and by medieval times had become a symbol of Christianity and the special flower of the Virgin Mary. Even today it is widely used to decorate churches.

In more recent times, the lily-lover's focus has switched from Europe to Asia, and particularly to China. The famous plant hunter, Ernest Henry Wilson, found *Lilium regale* growing in an inaccessible val-

RECOMMENDED VARIETIES FOR BEGINNERS

L. hansonii (orange-yellow turk's cap)
L. henryi (yellow turk's cap)
L. martagon (rose-purple, spotted turk's cap)
L. pyrenaicum (greenish-yellow turk's cap)
L. regale (white funnels flushed pink)
L. tigrinum also known as *L. lancifolium* (orange-red turk's cap)
'Black Dragon' (trumpets, white inside, dark red outside)
'Bright Star' (white cups with orange stripe)
'Casablanca' (large white cups)
'Citronella' (lemon to golden yellow)
'Connecticut King' (bright yellow cups)
'Enchantment' (orange-red cups with black spots)
'Green Dragon' (white cups streaked brown and green outside)
'Harlequin' strain (all colours)
'Pink Perfection' (pink trumpets)
'Star Gazer' (crimson-red with white border)

ley in tens of thousands – its heady fragrance must have been overpowering.

Fascinating flowers

There is a tremendous variation in lily flowers. Although always recognizable as lilies, they appear in no less than six different shapes.

Those that have bell-shaped flowers, such as *L. nanum*, have petals that are either straight or curve inwards towards the tips. In bowl-shaped flowers (*L. auratum*, for exam-

The nodding, scarlet turk's cap blooms of L. pumilum, *also known as* L. tenuifolium *(right) are among the smallest of all true lily flowers.*

INCREASING YOUR INVESTMENT

After a few years, if all goes well, your lilies should have spread into a large clump. To increase your stock, dig the clump up in autumn, and break it apart into groups of bulbs. Replant immediately, so that the bulbs will have time to grow new roots before winter comes.

If your lily produces bulbils in the leaf axils, or bulblets on the underground stem, detach these in autumn and replant immediately in a nursery bed. Keep them there for two years before moving to permanent quarters.

GROWING TIPS

Pat Brindley

ple), the petals are more widely spaced and slightly recurved or reflexed (that is, rolled back) at the tips.

Cup- or star-shaped flowers, as in the hybrid 'Bright Star', are similar but more compact, and may or may not roll back at the tips. *L. regale* has funnel-shaped flowers. These are more tubular, flaring out towards the mouth. Trumpet-shaped flowers, like those of the popular Easter lily (*L. longiflorum*) are the same but longer and narrower.

Perhaps the best-known flower form is the turk's cap or martagon type, with strongly recurved petals – sometimes so much so that the flower becomes actually ball shaped and the long, graceful stamens are fully exposed.

This is not the end of the lily flowers' variety. While some are pendent, nodding their heads to the ground, others point outwards, or upwards to face the sun.

Many lilies add to their attractiveness with a rich fragrance, although some, such as *L. pyrenaicum*, actually smell rather unpleasant.

Most lilies flower in midsummer, but some flower earlier or later, so it is perfectly possible to have a succession of lilies blooming in your garden for almost half the year.

The flowers are produced at the top of a single upright stem, grouped in pairs or bunches. The number of flowers can be up to 50 or more, and they appear over a period of several weeks. They vary in size from the modest 2.5cm/1in blooms of *L. pumilum* to those produced by the golden-rayed lily (*L. auratum*), which can reach 30cm/12in across. Lily leaves are stalkless and relatively insignificant, growing in whorls or scattered evenly up the stem.

True and false lilies

All true lilies – members of the genus *Lilium* – grow from bulbs. This distinguishes them

Many years of work by dedicated lily lovers have produced some truly spectacular varieties and hybrids. The tiger lily (L. lancifolium syn. L. tigrinum), with its large, spotted turk's cap flowers, has long been a favourite; the variety L. l. splendens (above) has even bigger flowers in a brighter shade of orange.

The golden yellow cups of the hybrid 'Connecticut King' (left) are held aloft on stems some 1m/3ft high with their faces to the sun.

PERFECT PARTNERS

Gillian Beckett

The pale, shapely blooms of the Madonna lily are an excellent foil for colourful border plants. Here they set off the pale pinks and yellows of *Alstroemeria* 'Ligtu'.

LILIES IN CONTAINERS

Growing lilies in containers means that you can put them somewhere inconspicuous while they are developing, and move them into the limelight when in flower. Do not forget, though, that very large containers become too heavy to move once filled with compost.

Container growing also means that you have full control over the type of soil, and the position, to suit the lily's needs.

Add interest by planting a small companion plant around the lily – this will help keep the bulbs cool by shading the soil. Choose small annuals in a colour that complements the lily. Use white flowers, or grey-leaved plants such as senecio, to cool down a very brightly coloured lily.

Andrew Lawson

from plants like arum lily (*Zantedeschia*) and day lily (*Hemerocallis*). The bulbs are different from ordinary ones like those of the daffodil, having no papery covering, and consisting of a large number of fleshy scales.

Like the flowers, the bulb shapes vary – some are round and some shaped like the rhizome of an iris, while others produce chains of round bulbs linked by stolons.

Many lilies produce bulblets on the underground part of the stem, just above the bulb. A few produce bulbils where the leaves join the stem. Both can be used for propagation.

Where to plant

Lilies can be grown in many parts of the garden. Those that like full sun thrive in herbaceous or mixed borders, or in tubs. Those that prefer dappled shade are excellent for planting under trees, or can be used among shrubs to provide

Photos Horticultural

The funnel-shaped flowers of L. regale *are pink in bud, but open to a dazzling white (far left).*

'Enchantment' (left) has become a popular cut flower in recent years. Very like the tiger lily in colour, it is distinguished by its upturned, cup-shaped flower form.

The flowers of L. pyrenaicum *are lovely to look at (below left), but many find their scent unpleasant.*

Cardiocrinum giganteum (below), sold as a giant lily, produces a tall, flamboyant flower spike, then the bulb dies, producing offsets that will flower again in five years.

Tania Midgley

LILY CLASSIFICATIONS

Botanists divide the vast family of lilies into nine groups. The largest contains all the original species lilies found growing wild in different parts of the world, many of which are hardy and easily grown. The other eight contain the huge number (over 3,500 registered!) of hybrids – some hardy, some tender – which have developed by crossing and recrossing the species plants. The six main groups readily available to gardeners are listed below.

● **Asiatic hybrids** are generally compact, no more than 1.2m/4ft high. Many are unfussy as to soil and aspect. The Mid-century hybrids contained within this group are especially easy.

● **Martagon and *L. hansonii* hybrids** all have small, pendent, turk's cap flowers and do best in partial shade.

● **Candidum and *L. chalcedonicum* hybrids** have long, pendent, trumpet-shaped flowers.

● **Bellingham hybrids** do best on acid soil in semi-shade.

● **Trumpet and Aurelian hybrids** mostly have large, trumpet-shaped flowers. They prefer rich, lime-free soil and semi-shade.

● **Oriental hybrids** have striking white, crimson or pink flowers, but may not be quite so hardy as others; they are good subjects for tubs in the sun.

Don Wildridge

ary. Good air circulation is needed, to avoid fungal infection – but strong winds can badly damage the plants.

Observe the recommended planting depth exactly, and mark the spot with a stick so that you remember where they are. (Also do this when the stems die down in autumn, so there is no risk of digging up or damaging the precious bulbs while they are dormant.)

In winter, avoid frost damage to lilies in borders by mulching thickly with peat; bring containers into a frost-free shed. Protect bulbs from snails and slugs, and keep watch for aphids, which can spread virus diseases.

colour when these have finished flowering.

Plant lilies singly or in groups of three, in a spot where they can be admired at close quarters – though of course the really tall ones will need to go in the back of a border. If you grow several varieties, for the best effect keep them apart from one another.

Secrets of success

It is best to buy lily bulbs from specialist nurseries by mail order. They are normally despatched between autumn and spring – if the ground is frozen, plunge the bulbs into moist peat and wait. It is best not to choose a lily just for its looks – you **must** be able to give it the right conditions.

Most lilies offered by nurseries thrive in free-draining but not dry soil – work coarse sand or grit into heavier soils before planting lilies – and in sun or partial shade. Make sure that those preferring alkaline or acid soils get what they want – plant them in tubs if necess-

SUPERLILY

Some lily nurseries also offer *Cardiocrinum giganteum*, a species of giant lily. The bulbs are among the most expensive, but a giant lily in full flower is a real talking point. The stem grows to 2.4m/8ft high or more, and each one can carry 25 flowers. These are 15-20cm/6-8in long, pure white trumpets, striped reddish purple inside, and give way to decorative seed heads.

GARDEN NOTES

Primulas

Hardy primulas come in all shapes and sizes – woodland primroses, colourful bedding polyanthus, pretty cowslips and many more.

Primulas range in colour from white to almost black, taking in clear hues, delicate pastels and more subtle, dusky shades. There are bi-colour and tri-colour flowers, with contrasting central 'eyes' and petal edges. They can be single, semi-double or double; shaped like discs, trumpets, bells or even rosebuds; upright or nodding; and carried singly, in tiers, clusters or spikes.

These charming, easy-to-grow perennials form low clumps or rosettes with deciduous or semi-evergreen leaves.

A woodland carpet of many colours. Left to spread naturally, multi-hued polyanthus (right) will form a glorious mat together with other low-growing naturalized springtime plants such as grape hyacinths and forget-me-nots.
Primula auricula 'Broadwell Gold' (below) looks eye catching in any rockery with its prominent drumstick flowerheads. The crinkled petals sit on a leafless stem which grows to 15cm/6in.

Tania Midgley

Harry Smith

The showy, five-petalled, sometimes fragrant flowers appear mainly in spring and summer. They grow on leafless stems, that can reach up to a height of 90cm/36in.

The hundreds of species and varieties are grouped according to various botanical specifications. The most popular and reliable are:

Auricula This widely grown common group has fleshy leaves, often covered with a powdery white coating.

The tall cowslip Primula veris (right), with its vivid red flowers, makes a striking statement in a bed of green waterside plants. This neat clump-forming perennial likes boggy conditions and brings a welcome burst of colour in spring.

S & O Mathews

They produce round flower clusters of subtly coloured blooms in late spring and some are bi- or tri-coloured, 15cm/6in high and across. Includes most of the alpine varieties.

Candelabra A very popular

upright type with long-toothed leaves. Up to eight tiers, or whorls, of mainly yellow, orange, pink or red flowers, 60-75cm high x 45cm spread (24-30in x 18in), including *clump-forming japonica*. Flowers in late spring-early summer.

Polyanthus – Primulas in this group have wrinkled, semi-evergreen leaves and profuse clusters of bright, yellow-eyed spring flowers in many colours, including blue. Height and spread: 15-30cm x 15-30cm/6-12in x 6-12in.

Vernalis – These generally have crinkly, toothed leaves and are more commonly known as primroses. Profuse flowers usually on single, short stems appear in spring. Includes the primrose, cowslip

Avoid any with pale, discoloured or wilted leaves, and those with few leaves. Look for plants with lots of flower buds and just a hint of flower colour to show you exactly what you are getting. Avoid plants in full flower because, however lovely and tempting, they will soon finish their display.

You need good clumps of colour to make an impact – plant five or seven roots of a single type together. A mixture of 'one of each' looks very 'spotty'.

Formal bedding polyanthus should be planted 20cm/8in apart in both directions.

Where to grow

Border primulas, such as candelabra and 'drumstick' types look lovely massed in shady beds and borders, by the edge of streams or pools, or in bog gardens. Primroses are ideal in drifts under trees or hedges; cowslips are perfect in rough grass. Polyanthus and drumstick primulas are traditionally used in formal bedding schemes, as edging, in window boxes and containers.

Rich soil that does not dry out is best. Alpine species need well-drained, gritty soil and those used in borders need more moisture. Most of them prefer semi-shade. Polyanthus and some alpines need sun, but not hot, dry conditions.

Planting primulas

You can plant primulas at any time except when the ground is waterlogged or frozen. First, dig over the area, removing weeds and adding well rotted garden compost or sterilized compost plus grit for alpines. Dig a hole to the depth of the plant's pot and, if the soil is dry, fill the hole with water and allow to drain. Water the plant, remove from its pot and place in the hole, making sure the top of the rootball is level with the soil. Firm in well and water again. Finally, sprinkle a little fertilizer around the plant to encourage strong, healthy growth. If planting in

Candelabra (left) 'P. japonica' is so called because of its dainty whorls of flowers which are spaced apart on a tall stem. Grown in clumps, these elegant primulas make a bold bank of colour in the spring months. This type of primula grows to 45cm/18in high and needs a constantly moist soil in partial shade to flourish well.

John Glover

and wine-purple 'Wanda'. 5-25cm/2-10in x 15-30cm/6-12in.

Buying and choosing

Buy primulas or polyanthus between early autumn and mid-spring. With dormant plants, you have to rely on the reputation of the garden centre, but save the label in case the plant fails to grow in spring or something unexpected comes up. When they are in growth, choose leafy plants.

PLANT PROFILE

Suitable site and soil: different species have different requirements. Border varieties love moisture retentive, humus-rich soil in a partially shaded area. Alpine species must have well-drained sandy or gritty soil in a sunny position. Do not allow conditions to become too dry.

Planting: plant in spring or autumn when the ground is moist, but not waterlogged or frozen. It also helps to water the plant in its pot before planting into position. Add peat at planting time. Water well and sprinkle with fertilizer.

Cultivation and care: do not allow primulas to dry out, particularly while in growth. Dead-head faded blooms. In spring, apply mulch. Divide clumps to prevent overcrowding.

Propagation: clump-forming varieties can be lifted and divided every three to four years in spring; primrose (vernalis) types, every two years. Place in new position in enriched soil.

Take 5cm/2in cuttings from auricula types in summer, plant in a mixture of peat and sand and over-winter in a cold frame or under glass. Plant out in position next spring.

Pests and diseases: in the main, trouble free, although caterpillars are partial to the leaves. Grey mould may appear if conditions are damp during growth. There is no cure and affected plants must be burned to prevent further infection.

Shapes and sizes: there are many varieties of primula. **Auricula** may be alpines or border plants. The flowers are grouped in an umbel on a stem above the foliage. **Candelabra**, as their name suggests, have tiered whorls of flowers on the stem. **Drumstick** types have a pompon of flowers on top of the stem. **Polyanthus** have profuse clusters of yellow-eyed flowers on erect stems.

Insight Picture Library

The most distinctive feature of many primulas is their bright central 'eyes' in contrasting colours. Shown here (above) to spectacular effect, this variety 'Insight' has deep red petals which compliment its yellow, winking star-like eyes.

Among a bed of brightly coloured polyanthus, this Primula vulgaris 'Viridiflora' (below) would hold its own with its unusual, exquisite green flowers. Each flower is borne on a single stem, surrounded by oval leaves.

David Russell/Garden Picture Library

Pat Brindley

Blooms in blue: this primrose (right) has no contrasting central eye, but boasts beautifully delicate double flowers and petals tinged with white. Falling in the vulgaris group, these primulas grow to a neat mound which reaches a height and width of 15cm/6in.

Photos Horticultural

Pat Brindley

The traditional soft yellow primrose, Primula vulgaris (above), looks most at home when set with other 'natural woodland' flowers like delicate purple violas. A moist, well-drained bank in partial shade provides the perfect conditions.

Primulas of the auricula group produce fragrant flowers carried in an umbel on a stem. This golden-hued variety (below) can grow up to 15cm/6in. Unlike the crinkly leaves of other primulas, these plants are smooth-leafed, often with a fine powdery surface.

TWELVE OF THE BEST PRIMULAS

Name	Type	Height x width	Flower
'Crescendo' F1 hybrids	Polyanthus	20cm/8in x 20cm/8in	various colours, large blooms
'Posy series' F1 hybrids	Polyanthus	7.5cm/3in x 7.5cm/3in	various colours and bi-colours
P. alpicola (moonlight primula)	Sikkimensis	30-60cm/1-2ft x 30cm/1ft	fragrant, creamy white to yellow
P. auricula ('Dusty Miller')	Auricula	15cm/6in x 15cm/6in	various colours and multi-colours
P. beesiana	Candelabra	60cm/2ft x 45cm/1½ft	reddish purple, yellow eye
P. bulleyana	Candelabra	60-75cm/2-2½ft x 45cm/1½ft	golden yellow to orange red
P. denticulata	Drumstick	30cm/1ft x 25cm/10in	pale lilac to deep purple, yellow eye
P. japonica (Japanese primrose)	Candelabra	60-75cm/2-2½ft x 45cm/1½ft	various colours, most with yellow eye
P. florindae (giant cowslip)	Sikkimensis	60-120cm/2-4ft x 60cm/2ft	fragrant, pale-to-deep yellow
P. veris (cowslip)	Vernalis	15-25cm/6-10in x 15cm/6in	fragrant, bright yellow, orange eye
P. vulgaris (primrose)	Vernalis	15cm/6in x 15cm/6in	pale yellow
'Wanda'	Vernalis	10cm/4in x 10cm/4in	wine-purple

Primula denticulata 'Alba' (right) is a beautiful example of the perfectly formed 'drumstick' variety. Sturdy stems that reach up to 30cm/1ft are topped by dense pompons of petals. The leaves, which fan around the stems in dense clumps, are 'toothed' with softly jagged edges.

Gillian Beckett

autumn, it is better to use slow-release fertilizer such as bone meal to prepare the plant for its major flowering period.

Moisture loving

Water primulas whenever the soil becomes dry. Mulch around plants with damp peat in spring, to smother weeds and retain soil moisture. Remove faded flowers to encourage further blooms. Lift and divide clump-forming types every three to four years, vernalis types every two years, as this will prevent overcrowding.

You can lift bedding primulas after flowering and replant them in an out-of-the-way spot until the following autumn.

Alpine primulas dislike cold, wet soil, so work a layer of grit around and under the plants in autumn to help keep their crowns dry. Place a horizontal pane of glass (across brick supports) above the plant to help prevent rot, while allowing air to circulate.

Many primulas die back in hot summers, but sprout again once cooler, autumn weather sets in, so don't worry if your plant temporarily disappears!

Plentiful plants

Divide established clumps after flowering. With a hand fork or trowel, lift the clump and gently prise apart the roots into several sections. Replant in a new, ready-prepared spot, or enrich the existing soil with a light sprinkling of all-purpose fertilizer, dug in before replanting.

Auriculas and other dwarf and mat-forming types of primula are propagated by 2.5-5cm/1-2in cuttings or by small rooted shoots. These are taken in summer and placed in trays of loam-based compost, overwintered in a cold frame, then

Pat Brindley

PERFECT PARTNERS

Polyanthus look lovely alongside tulips, daffodils, hyacinths, and wallflowers because they provide the horizontal ground cover and low-level interest needed around upright-growing bulbs.

In moist borders and bog gardens, primulas associate well with ferns, hostas, arum, marsh marigold, lady's mantle, astilbe and iris. In moist, peaty soil, they complement azaleas or rhododendrons.

In rockeries and sink gardens, grow primulas with saxifrage, aubrieta, fritillaria, anemone, alyssum, in sun or shade, according to type.

Although colourful and eye-catching on their own, primulas can be set off to great effect when set with other plants. Here, the stately candelabra Primula japonica rises above Montia sibirica in a woodland setting.

Eric Chrchton

PRIMULA POSIES

You or your children can bring a breath of spring into your home by picking a pretty posy of primulas from your garden.

Picked with their leaves, they look best in a small container. Cluster them together in a wine glass, milk jug or pretty cup for an informal effect.

Polyanthus are ideal for miniature displays. To keep them fresh, prick gently just below the flower head to release air bubbles, then give them a long drink before arranging the stems.

Auriculas will last longer if at first they are left for several hours in a basin of deep, warm water.

Brian Carter/Garden Picture Library

PROJECT — A PRIMULA PLANTER

A prettily designed basketful of primulas will brighten any corner. Cut up a black bin liner and use it to line a wicker basket. Pierce a few drainage holes. (To help drainage put some pieces of broken polystyrene at the bottom – this will be much lighter than pieces of broken clay pots.) Fill the basket three-quarters full with moist potting compost. Water primulas then remove from their pots. Arrange them in the basket, add more compost and firm them in. Water the primulas in well.

A wicker basket makes a pretty, portable container for a colourful collection of primulas on a patio or balcony.

Primula 'Wanda' (left) makes a tumbling crimson carpet. One of the primrose types, it prefers a woodland-like setting.

For striking but neat swatches of colour in spring borders, try the hardy Primula denticulata (right) with its bold spheres of bright pink petals.

Mix an assortment of Primula vulgaris together (below) for a long-lasting cushion of colour. Divide in the autumn.

planted out the next spring.

Species can be grown from seed, but named varieties do not breed true to type. Rinse the seed in warm water, to remove the natural germination inhibitor, then simple 'surface sow' – scattering the fine seed on the surface of damp, peat-based compost. Cover with a pane of glass as described above and keep cool, shaded and moist until seedlings appear, then remove the glass. When the seedlings are large enough to handle, pot up into trays or boxes of John Innes No 1 compost. Keep the young plants cool and shaded, and plant them out in early autumn or spring. Do not plant them in waterlogged soil.

Any problems?

Primulas are generally trouble-free. But here is what to do if the following occurs:
- If aphids or greenfly attack flowering shoots, try removing them with soapy water.
- If caterpillars eat the leaves, pick them off individually if there are only a few, or spray or dust with derris.
- If grey mould appears or if the leaves develop orange or brown spots, remove and burn diseased leaves and spray the plant with a suitable fungicide.
- If any viral diseases occur, dig the plant up and burn it to prevent any infection.

Radiant Roses

The rose is one of the most versatile of plants, with literally hundreds of varieties offering soft-petalled, fragrant blooms and stunning ornamental effects.

A rose bed need not be a rigid, regimental affair; informal plantings of mixed varieties (above) can produce a dazzling kaleidoscope of colour throughout the season.

The rose has attracted an army of specialist growers over the last few centuries. Their enthusiasm has created an almost limitless variety of plants with a wealth of flower shapes, colours and scents.

Within the broad categories of modern garden roses, old garden roses and wild roses, there are rampant climbers, bushy shrubs and ground-cover varieties. Some have delicate single flowers with 5-8 petals, some semi-double blooms with 10-25, while others produce full double roses with more than 40.

Many modern varieties carry one flower to a stem, while others, the floribundas, produce clusters or trusses of smaller blooms; there are also several miniature varieties.

Roses can provide floral display in a mixed bed or stand alone as a specimen plant in a patio tub. Climbers and ramblers can screen the garden shed or cloak an archway in colour and fragrance. Ground cover varieties may be the answer on a difficult bank, while its thorns make the rose particularly effective in a barrier hedge. Miniature varieties can do well in a window box.

This abundance means that the key to using roses as part of a creative plan in the garden is first to decide what effect you require and then to choose the varieties whose colours and growing habits best suit what you have in mind.

A special rose bed

Rose enthusiasts usually prefer to keep them apart from other plants, so they can lavish attention on them, and a separate rose bed is the best place to display many of the modern varieties, grown as shrubs or standards.

Hybrid tea roses are best suited to a formal rose bed. They produce well shaped double flowers, typically one bloom on each flowering stem. Their elegance makes them the perfect choice if you aim to fill the rooms of your house with bowls of cut flowers.

If you prefer a less formal look, you can soften the appearance of a rose bed by underplanting standards with border plants such as forget-me-nots and lady's mantle (*Alchemilla mollis*.) The soft, delicate foliage and host of small flowers that characterize these plants soften the edges of a bed and provide interest when the roses are not in bloom.

A standard rose, either with a round, bushy head or trained into a weeping shape, can be used as a central focus in a formal herb garden. These

specimen plants are very useful as centrepieces in any circular bed, offering height and shape all year round and a cascade of scent and colour when in full seasonal bloom.

Good bedfellows

In contrast to the hybrid tea varieties, **old garden roses** grow in a very informal way,

blending harmoniously into all kinds of mixed shrub and herbaceous borders.

Many of these varieties have been grown for centuries, but can still offer a modern garden much to treasure. Gentler in style than the modern roses, their buds and flowers have a delicate beauty.

Rosa chinensis 'Mutabilis', also known as 'Tipo Ideale', for instance, produces papery flowers for much of the summer and bronze foliage in spring. Another eye-catching old rose is *R. gallica versicolor*, a variety that is at least 300 years old, whose petals are streaked with shades of pink.

Old roses tend to be available only from specialist growers, but they are well worth seeking out to soften and add interest to mixed bor-

Harry Smith Collection

Several varieties of rose give good ground cover. Rosa 'Pheasant' (below) produces masses of small pink semi-double flowers. Other 'game bird' roses give different colours; R. 'Grouse' is pale pink, and R. 'Partridge' white.

Eric Crichton

ders. Their foliage often makes a more dramatic contribution to a border than their flowers.

R. rubrifolia, for instance, produces short-lived and unspectacular blooms, but its almost thornless stems and leaves of pinky-grey earn it a place in many gardens. Grown next to a plant with silver

A collection of miniature roses makes an excellent, free-flowering subject for a container or a raised bed (above).

ROSES FOR EVERY PURPOSE

- For a formal rose garden choose the large-flowered hybrid tea rose *'Peace'* with its pink-tipped yellow petals.
- For an informal shrub border choose *'Iceberg'* or the red-flowered *'Fragrant Delight'*. Both are cluster-flowered roses.
- Choice climbing roses for a wall or screen include *'Zéphirine Drouhin'*, a thornless pink-flowered rose that flowers continously through the summer and has a deep fragrance. For a sunny effect choose *'Golden Showers'*.
- Rambling roses that can be trained over arches, fallen trees and across the front of a house include *'American Pillar'* with its deep red roses; the fragrant pink *'Albertine'* and the rampant *'Kiftsgate'*.
- If you prefer to try old garden roses in a mixed shrubbery *Rosa rubrifolia* offers pretty foliage and attractive hips.
- For hedges use the rugosa rose, *'Frau Dagmar Hartopp'*.
- Good ground cover roses include the Japanese rose, *'Nozomi'*, and *'Pheasant'* with masses of small flowers.

leaves, it makes a strong decorative focus. Both the filigree foliage of artemisia and the huge indented leaves of an ornamental artichoke, for example, provide a striking contrast to the delicate leaves of this old garden rose.

Containers

You do not need a bed of any kind to enjoy roses, which will happily grow in containers on a patio or balcony; some will grow in a window box. Wooden tubs make the best containers for all types of rose, from miniature to standard.

Make sure that any rose you choose for container cultivation is disease-resistant, as it will be more vulnerable in its tub than in the ground. For all-year interest, plant the container with trailing ivy, and in late spring add annual plants such as lobelia to make a froth of colour at the base.

Miniature roses, such as 'Baby Masquerade', which grows to 38cm/15in high, look well as the focal point of a tub. Small-flowered annual bedding plants chosen to complement the colour of the rose will

soften the edge of the container. Dwarf varieties can also be used in a window box, as a short-term house plant, as edging at the front of a border, or as a splash of colour on a small rockery.

Not all roses grow upwards. Some make spreading horizontal growth and are ideal ground cover. They provide a ready solution to a 'difficult' slope or bank, transforming it into a colourful, flower-strewn bed requiring the minimum of maintenance.

Floral carpets

The variety 'Nozomi', with its profusion of single pearly-pink blooms, is particularly suited to this purpose, as are 'Partridge' and 'Red Blanket', which are both smothered with flowers and boast disease-resistant leaves.

Weed the site carefully before planting, since the roses will not actually suppress weeds, and it is difficult to remove them from between the roses once established.

Roses can be used to mark out short internal hedges between parts of the garden. For

PERFECT PARTNERS

In a garden where space is short, the stems of a tall-growing shrub rose can act as a support for annual sweet peas, whose blooms will intertwine with those of the rose to make a living bouquet.

Carole Hellman/Garden Picture Library

MAINTENANCE

All roses should be kept well-watered until they are established. As their roots go deep, it should not be necessary to water them again except in long, dry spells. Water them direct from the spout of the can, held close to the ground. They should be fed in spring and the area round the stem mulched with compost or manure (do not let it come into direct contact with the stem).

Apart from this, old garden roses need very little attention, apart from dead-heading and removing diseased or damaged wood in spring. They do not need to be pruned like modern varieties, simply clipped back.

DON'T FORGET!

Eric Crichton

Many shrub roses, although classified as modern garden varieties, have the timeless appeal of old garden roses. The creamy-pink scented flowers, dense foliage and arching habit of R. 'Nevada' (above) make it an inspired choice for framing a garden gate.

Harry Smith Collection

Perderau-Thomas/Garden Picture Library

anything on a larger scale, a rose hedge tends to be rather too expensive.

Hedges and screens

The best choices for hedging are the *R. rugosa* varieties, which have a compact shape and flower repeatedly. Their bright, fat hips extend interest into the autumn and winter. Miniature roses make an interesting and attractive alternative to edging a formal herb garden or shrub border.

Rambling and climbing roses make the best screens, masking rubbish bins, unsightly downpipes or simply a dull wall. Both will grow quickly along a support. This can be a lattice of wires or trellis fixed to the wall, or a free standing screen over which the plants can be trained.

Roses are often the first choice for covering arches and pergolas. Rambling varieties, though they tend to have a short flowering season, pro-

vide good foliage cover; 'Albertine', with its heavy scent and attractive, full-blown flowers, is a favourite choice.

For more dramatic effect, climbers can be planted to sweep along rope swags trained from wooden pillars or formal tripods. On the pillars, they will thicken up and make a dense show of flowers; along the ropes they become a ribbon of linking colour.

Such effects take time to produce and require varieties

The Bourbon rose, R. 'Zéphirine Drouhin', has no thorns, which reduces its effectiveness as a barrier. However, it makes a fine, fragrant hedge for dividing up the garden (top).

A miniature rose can stand alone as a specimen plant in a pot or tub (above); where its perfectly-shaped flowers and foliage can be easily appreciated.

Roses can make fine border plants as here (right) where the floribunda 'August Seebauer' is combined with santolina to stunning effect.

Many roses have attractive hips, but those of R. rugosa (below) are especially fine, full and plump and set off to perfection by the variety's glossy, crinkled leaves.

Eric Crichton

Photos Horticultural

with a fairly rampant growth habit such as 'Schoolgirl', 'New Dawn' or 'Pink Perpetué'.

Fringe benefits

Roses offer so much in terms of colour and abundant flower that it is easy to overlook the plant's less obvious delights.

The seed-heads, or hips, of many varieties are attractive in their own right. Plump, sleek and scarlet, they stay on the plant throughout the winter. 'Frau Dagmar Hartopp', also sold as 'Frau Dagmar Hastrup', a rugosa rose that is good for hedging and for planting in a mixed shrub border, has round, fat hips, while *R.*

moyesii 'Geranium' has long, rich red ones.

The pretty hips of the grey-leaved *R. rubrifolia* make a welcome decorative addition to both the garden and the house in the depths of winter.

Moss roses originated as a chance sport from cabbage roses. Their mossy stems and buds are almost as stunning as the full blooms that follow. This effect is best seen in the beautifully-scented *R. centifolia* 'Muscosa'.

Scent

Fragrance can play a large part in choosing and siting a rose. Part of the traditional appeal of growing roses around a doorway is the heavenly scent which greets you when you open the door on a summer's evening.

Many of the old garden roses, such as the free-flowering 'Rose d'Amour' and 'Gloire de Dijon', otherwise known as 'Old Glory', also have delicious, evocative perfumes, while 'Zéphirine Drouhin' offers a sea of fragrant pink flowers.

For some rose-lovers, though, it is the thorns that are the attraction. *R. sericea pteracantha* is a spiny rose with filigree foliage. In the sunlight, its large red thorns give a very different kind of ornamental effect.

PROJECT

TRAINING A CLIMBER

The image of a rose clambering over a cottage wall and framing the door is deeply embedded in English country life, but in fact this may not be the perfect place to grow a rose. Beds right up against a wall often prove too dry for roses. The growth of their roots can be restricted, which makes them vulnerable to disease.

Climbing roses should be planted some 45cm/18in from

Michael Shoebridge

the wall. Lay the roots so that they slope away from the wall. Tie the lower parts of the stem into the

supports, laying the branches horizontally across the wall to encourage new shoots to grow upwards.

Shrub Roses

No garden is complete without a few shrub roses, the most versatile and easiest to grow of all the garden roses.

For many years shrub roses were thought of, particularly by rose specialists, as the poor relations of the rose family – probably because they require so little attention.

They are, however, ideal for the gardener who does not have hours to spend pruning and spraying. With virtually no fuss many will flower throughout the summer, often continuing when other shrubs have ceased to flower.

Shrub roses are such versatile plants they can be used almost anywhere. Usually they are quite large, 1.5m/5ft or more in height, and produce a mass of continuous blooms. They can be used in the shrub border, for hedging, or individually as specimen plants, set in the lawn for example.

Some varieties, with particularly graceful, arching stems, are ideally suited for the back of the herbaceous border. There are even low-growing varieties which provide excellent ground cover and help to suppress weeds.

The term shrub roses is used to describe a huge range of old and modern roses, which for convenience are divided into five groups; rugosas, hybrid musks, modern shrubs, ground cover and old fashioned.

Rugosas

Free from disease and luxuriant in growth, rugosa roses make large, dense, shapely shrubs which will grow in even the poorest soils.

One of the biggest and best is 'Roseraie de l'Hay', the traditional hedging rose, reaching 2.1m/7ft wide. Ideal for screening your garden from

Collections/Patrick Johns

the neighbours, it is a tough, vigorous grower with dense, apple-green foliage. The fragrance of the ruffled, wine-coloured flowers is sensational and you can expect repeat flowering right through into the autumn.

If you prefer a white flower, *R. rugosa* 'Alba' is a tough variety of the original species rose *Rosa rugosa*. The shrub is not quite as large as 'Roseraie de l'Hay', but the silky-textured flowers measuring 8cm/3in

across are produced in profusion throughout the summer. In the autumn, the flowers give way to huge orange hips. Use *R. rugosa* 'Alba' to form a hedge, or as an integral part of a shrub border.

Hybrid musks

Hybrid musks are graceful, arching shrubs which are best grown in a mixed border. Their real star quality is the abundant clusters of small flowers which persist right

Much of the appeal of modern shrub roses is encapsulated in the massive, spicily-perfumed double blooms – about 12cm/5in in diameter – of the free-flowering variety 'Constance Spry' (above), which appear in midsummer. The shrub itself is tall and arching, but will climb if it is well supported.

PLANT PROFILE

Suitable site and soil: Full sun but some varieties will tolerate shade; well-drained soil with lots of organic matter, although poorer soils tolerated.

Planting: Space the plants 1.5m/5ft apart; for hedging 1m/3ft apart. Add garden compost and bone meal to the planting hole.

Cultivation and care: Water in dry spells; mulch in spring and summer; prune only if shrub is misshapen or ceases to flower. Cutting back the shoots that have just flowered will encourage more flowers.

Propagation: Best left to the experts – buy as bare-root or container grown plants.

Pests and diseases: Mainly trouble-free although mildew can attack the old-fashioned varieties. Spray to remove aphids or allow natural predators to do their work.

through the autumn, up until the first frosts.

'Buff Beauty' is perhaps the most beautiful rose in this group. The warm, apricot-yellow flowers are full blown and slightly larger than some of the other hybrid musks. They are fragrant, and blooms appear in large trusses from midsummer onwards. The shrub itself is vigorous, and will even grow in a shady cor-ner or on poor soil. Eventually it will reach a height and spread of 1.5m/5ft.

Another favourite is 'Corne-lia', which actually looks its best in the autumn. Similar in size to 'Buff Beauty', it makes a good hedge with dense, dark green foliage. The flowers are pink, with a hint of apricot, and although small, appear in very pretty sprays with a deli-cate perfume.

Some of the best shrub roses have been developed by cross-ing modern bush roses with older, stronger species. The re-sult is a group of strong, healthy modern shrubs that thrive in most situations.

Modern shrubs

For the back of the border, 'Constance Spry' is a good choice. The arching stems, up to 1.8m/6ft tall, need some

'Roseraie de l'Hay' (above), like most of the rugosa roses, is a vigorous plant, soon making a good-sized shrub. The semi-double flowers are between red and purple in colour and have a strong, sweet scent.

'Boule de Neige' (right, above) is an old-fashioned variety. Its fragrant double flowers, 8cm/3in in diameter, sometimes have a hint of pink. They appear in late summer and early autumn.

The stunning carmine flowers of the arching old-fashioned rose, 'Mme Isaac Pereire' (right) are fully 15cm/6in across. The petals of the double blooms make a distinctive, quartered shape.

'Pink Bells', also known as 'Poulbells' (left), makes excellent ground cover, with dense foliage and great quantities of small (2.5cm/1in across) flowers. Here, it has filled to overflowing a stone container.

Photos Horticultural

Andrew Lawson

RECOMMENDED VARIETIES

Rugosas
'Blanc Double de Coubert' (white semi-double)
'Fru Dagmar Hastrup', also known as 'Frau Dagmar Hartopp' (pink single)
'Robusta' (scarlet, single)
Rosa rugosa 'Alba' (white single)
'Roseraie de l'Hay' (crimson-purple semi-double)
'Scabrosa' (crimson single)

Hybrid musks
'Buff Beauty' (apricot double)
'Cornelia' (copper-apricot double)
'Felicia' (salmon-pink double)
'Moonlight' (cream semi-double)
'Penelope' (pale pink semi-double)

Modern shrubs
'Constance Spry' (rose-pink double)
'Gertrude Jekyll' (pink double)
'Graham Thomas' (yellow double)
'Jacqueline du Pré' (white semi-double)
'Scarlet Fire' (scarlet single)

Ground cover
'Grouse' (pale pink single)
'Partridge' (white single)
'Pheasant' (pink double)
'Pink Bells' (pink double)
'Red Bells' (red double)

Old fashioned
'Boule de Neige' (white double bourbon)
'General Kleber' (mauve-pink double moss)
'Fantin-Latour' (blush-pink double centifolia)
'Mme. Isaac Pereire' (carmine-pink double bourbon)
'Rosa Mundi' (striped crimson/pink semi-double gallica).

support from a back wall or fence. It is especially prized for its huge, richly scented, rose-pink double blooms which appear in midsummer.

'Jacqueline du Pré' is another modern shrub well worth growing. The white, musky-scented flowers have frilly edges and go on appearing through summer and autumn. The bush itself is well rounded, reaching 1.8m/6ft high, and can be grown in a group or as an individual

Photos Horticultural

specimen plant.

Several shrub roses have a low growing habit which makes them ideal for ground cover. Plant them wherever there is a space in the border and they will keep down the weeds all year long.

The sprawling growth of 'Pheasant' makes it an ideal rose for covering slopes or trailing over low walls. It spreads to 3m/10ft wide and produces deep rose-pink blooms in large trusses.

Another variety, 'Pink Bells' provides cover with its dark green foliage, which forms a dense mat 1.2m/4ft wide, rather than its pink pompon-shaped blooms, which appear in mid to late summer.

Old fashioned

The old-fashioned group includes some of the most romantic old roses, grown in French and English gardens over the last three centuries. There are literally hundreds to choose from but a few can be singled out for their reliability and charm.

For scent and full-blown old fashioned blooms, 'Mme. Issac

'Rosa Mundi' (R. gallica 'Versicolor') is unmistakable. Its semi-double, rather flat flowers are striped with swirling shades of pink. The blooms are not large, just 5cm/2in in diameter, and they are not as strongly scented as many of the other old-fashioned roses, but their carnival colouring has earned the bushy, compact shrub a place in the garden for more than five centuries.

PERFECT PARTNERS

It's a myth that roses have to grow on their own. Shrub roses with their arching branches look even better if the borders are interplanted with other tall growing plants or edged with smaller ones. Grey or silver leaves and plants with blue, pink or mauve flowers look particularly good with shrub roses (right).

For edging, try sage (*Salvia officinalis*), lavender (*Lavandula* 'Munstead'), catmint (*Nepeta × faassenii*) or geranium (*Geranium* 'Johnson's Blue').

Plants suitable for interplanting include foxglove (*Digitalis purpurea*), rosemary (*Rosmarinus officinalis*), regal lily (*Lilium regale*) and everlasting pearl (*Anaphalis triplinervis*).

Collections/Patrick Johns

Pereire' is hard to beat. The branching stems reach 2.1m/7ft, so it should be grown at the back of the border or as a climber, using a fence or wall for support. The huge, informal carmine pink flowers have one of the most penetrating perfumes of all the old roses.

'Rosa Mundi' (*R. gallica* 'Versicolor') cannot possibly be mistaken for any other rose: its striking blooms have dark pink striping on a pale pink background. It is one of the oldest varieties now in existence and was probably used in 16th century gardens as an eye-catching low hedge – it grows to a neat, compact height and spread of 1.2m/4ft.

Planting and care

Shrub roses are sold either as 'bare-root' or 'container-grown' plants. Bare-rooted plants are often sold in supermarkets, but they should only be planted in the winter. Container-grown shrubs from garden centres or nurseries can be planted at any time.

Once planted, the care of your shrub rose could not be easier. Keep new plants well-watered, particularly during dry spells.

A mulch of well-rotted manure or garden compost applied around, but not touching, the stem in the autumn and spring will help retain the moisture in the soil and supply some nutrients.

Most shrub roses do not need pruning. However, after some years, the shrubs may get leggy or cease to flower well. In that case, the side shoots should be shortened by a third in winter. Roses used for hedging should be pruned as if they were individual bushes; this does not apply to rugosas, which should be lightly clipped with shears.

Harry Smith Collection

The moss roses are all hybrids or sports of R. centifolia *'Muscosa'*, distinguished by their fragrance and by the resinous, mossy glands on the sepals. *'General Kleber'* (above) is a particularly mossy variety with fully double blooms.

Photos Horticultural

In summer, 'Buff Beauty' (left) is smothered in double flowers ranging from pale buff to apricot in colour; in autumn, there are further flushes of flowers, though of a much less prolific nature. Though not as strongly perfumed as other hybrid musk roses, there is some consolation in its handsome, glossy foliage.

Miniature Roses

Gardeners find roses irresistible for their beauty and long flowering season. Miniatures have the same charms, plus the appeal of all things tiny.

The small size of many new gardens, and the increasing trend towards container planting, have led to a considerable increase in the popularity of miniature roses. Their tiny, dainty flowers have an appeal all of their own, and the small-sized plants – sometimes no more than 20cm/8in high – enable rose lovers to plant a pleasing selection where there is no room for ordinary full-size rose bushes.

Miniatures offer everything desirable in a rose – they are all repeat flowering, with a long season of bloom, and many are fragrant. The varieties available offer all the range of beautiful colours found in their larger cousins; reds, oranges, pinks, whites, yellows, lilac, bi-colours and even a near-green. The flowers are almost always double, and the plants themselves, despite their delicate appearance, are perfectly hardy.

The term miniature rose encompasses two distinct types: true miniatures and slightly larger plants that are sometimes catalogued as patio roses. There are also a few climbing miniature roses, and some varieties are also available as standards, growing a single straight stem about 30cm/1ft high.

Potted history

The miniature rose is not a new introduction – they were very popular in Victorian days, but gradually fell out of fashion and had all but disappeared by 1900.

Then, in 1918, a Major Roulet happened on a tiny pot-grown rose in Switzerland, which became known as *Rosa rouletii*. From this small beginning came the legions of present-day miniature roses.

Miniature roses are extremely popular in the United States, where they are used as house plants. In Britain, they do not succeed very well indoors, and many people became disillusioned with them.

Photos Horticultural

Many miniature roses are versions of well-known varieties; the carnival colouring of 'Baby Masquerade' mimics that of its grown-up sister.

The glossy foliage of 'Snow Carpet', also known as 'Maccarpe' (right) makes dense ground cover, and it flowers into the autumn.

The delightful double pink flowers of 'Pompon de Paris' (far right) were favourites of the Victorians.

Harry Smith Collection

The razmataz of the semi-double blooms of 'Stars 'n' Stripes' (right) would probably be overwhelming in a full-size rose, but makes for an appealingly colourful, candy-striped focus in a miniature form.

Harry Smith Collection

The reason is that the plants are raised differently. In the USA they are grown from cuttings, which makes them slow-growing and not very hardy, but guarantees they will remain small. In Britain the plants are generally grafted on to rootstocks of larger roses. This makes them hardier, faster-growing, and suited to life outdoors – but also means they can eventually grow undesirably large.

Ancient and modern

As with full-size roses, some miniature varieties have been in cultivation for a very long time. The bright pink 'Pompon de Paris', for example, was very popular in Victorian times. Others date back to the 1940s, but most of the big sellers are modern roses, produced by hybridists in the 1970s and 1980s. They are very fond of naming their babies after British TV personalities – if you wish you can buy 'Anna Ford', 'Angela Rippon' and 'Penelope Keith'.

One of the very latest patio roses is 'Queen Mother', launched in 1990 to celebrate Her Majesty's 90th birthday. This has semi-double flowers

---

PLANT PROFILE

Suitable site and soil
Well-prepared fertile soil in full sun.
Planting Buy container-grown roses for planting in spring or early summer, or bare root stock for planting from the beginning of autumn to late winter. Place the plants 20cm/8in to 40cm/15in apart, depending on the effect required.
Cultivation and care Treat as ordinary roses, but don't forget to water well in dry weather as they have much smaller root systems and so dry out faster. Plants grown in pots and tubs may need watering twice a day in warm weather. Feed frequently with liquid fertilizer. Snip off dead blooms to encourage further flowering. Prune lightly at the beginning of spring – just

remove any dead wood and trim plant to desired shape. Plants can be brought indoors temporarily when in flower if desired, but should be promptly returned to the garden after they have finished flowering.
Propagation Take 7.5cm/3in cuttings from new growth in early autumn. Put several in a pot and keep out of direct sunlight. When new growth appears, pot up separately in 7.5cm/3in pots. Keep indoors until spring, then plant out or keep in pots – cuttings make good house plants.
Pests and diseases Watch for aphids and spray as soon as any appear. Like other roses, miniatures may also suffer from mildew and black spot. Spray at the first signs of disease – remove and burn all black-spotted leaves.

VERTICAL INTEREST

Use the climbing varieties of miniature rose to provide vertical interest where space is extremely limited and a regular climbing rose would soon need drastic pruning.

Perhaps the best one is 'Pink Cameo', also known as 'Climbing Cameo', which has very small, rich rose-pink flowers. It will only reach about 1.5m/5ft. 'Climbing Pompon de Paris', sometimes listed as 'Climbing Rouletii', is also pretty, with very small, bright pink flowers, but its second flush of flowers may be disappointing. This reaches up to 2.4m/8ft.

BRIGHT IDEAS

Tania Midgley

Photos Horticultural

across, but can sometimes be as big as 5cm/2in, and are almost always double.

Like their big sisters, miniatures produce flowers of varying shape and habit of growth. Depending on their parentage they may resemble miniature floribundas, growing in clusters, or tiny hybrid teas with high-centred blooms: many have rosette or pompon-type flowers. Some are mildly fragrant, but many of the new ones have no scent. The leaves are similar to those of big roses, but in proportion to the size of the plant, and the stems are usually prickly.

There are also patio roses, larger and somewhere between a miniature and a floribunda rose in character. Their average height is around 45cm/18in, and they have a neat, bushy habit of growth. Some nurseries do not list patio roses separately from miniatures, so check heights carefully when buying or you may end up with something which is three times larger than you had envisaged.

Buying miniatures

As they become popular, more garden centres are stocking a selection of miniature and patio roses. But for a really good choice you need to go to a specialist rose nursery, or send away for a catalogue so you can buy by mail order.

If possible see plants in bloom before buying, or at least in a colour photograph – they vary a lot in character, and what appeals to one person may not please another. For example, a popular patio rose, 'Chelsea Pensioner', is described as deep scarlet with gold shading at the base of the petals. In real life what you see is a startling mixture of scarlet and pink, because the flowers fade as they age.

Using miniatures

Miniature roses have a long flowering season, coming into bloom in midsummer and car-

Peter McHoy

in a delightful soft pink shade, and a very dainty, delicate appearance. If you are looking for something really unusual, there's even a pale, creamy green-flowered miniature – it's called 'Green Diamond'.

Little and large

A truly miniature rose grows no more than 20-30cm/8-12in tall – a few are listed as reaching only 15cm/6in. The flowers are usually about 2.5cm/1in

Harry Smith Collection

The distinction between miniature varieties and patio roses is not clear-cut; 'Dresden Doll' (above) is listed as a miniature in most catalogues, but a patio rose in others.

Miniature roses are versatile performers. Patio roses in containers make excellent specimen plants for a patio (above left), while several genuine miniature varieties make a vigorous show in a raised bed (below left).

'Yellow Doll' (below) is a genuine miniature, but there is nothing small or self-effacing about its magnificent double yellow blooms.

Harry Smith Collection

CAREFUL PLANTING

Plant your miniature roses with great care, otherwise they will never flourish.

Container grown Dig a hole in moist soil large enough for the container plus a 7.5cm/3in layer of proprietary planting mixture or moist peat all round and underneath. Do not use garden soil as roots raised in peat-based compost in the container may not move out into it. The top of the container should be at ground level. Gently slit and remove the container; do not break up compost around the roots. Set on the planting mixture and fill the space all round. Firm down well and water in.

Bare root Make a hole broad enough to give the roots plenty of room and deep enough to allow the bump where the grafted plants joins the rootstock to be 2.5cm/1in below ground. Fill with proprietary planting mixture and tread firmly. Keep moist until established.

DON'T FORGET!

rying on right until the first frosts strike. They are also extremely versatile.

Use them to create a small-scale rose garden, ideally in a raised bed so that they are closer to the eye. A mixture of true miniatures with the larger patio roses at the back or in the centre will give you the height gradation that makes a bed look as though it is professionally laid out.

Rockery roses

Alternatively, you can put some miniatures in a rockery to give interest in summer when many of the alpine flowers are long gone.

True miniatures, closely planted, make excellent edgings for conventional borders, while the slightly larger patio roses are recommended for container planting. However, once again it is a matter of scale, and a lot depends on the size of the container. Both sizes are ideal for beds and containers around a patio, where they can be seen at close quarters and really appreciated.

The one thing **not** to do with miniatures is mix them up with larger plants, especially full-size roses, or their small-scale charms will be much overshadowed and lost.

Exotic Daylilies

The exotic, lily-like flowers and decorative arching foliage of the daylilies contribute rich colour and sculptural shape to summer plantings.

The daylily is appropriately named: its flowers share the flared trumpet shape of the lily, and make their triumphant display only for a day. Yet, though each beautiful bloom is short-lived, the profusion of exotic flowers opening in succession over several weeks makes an invaluable show of colour throughout the summer months.

Daylilies all belong to the genus *Hemerocallis*. They are hardy herbaceous perennials, some semi-evergreen, and belong to the same family as the true lilies. The foliage is strap-shaped, like huge daffodil leaves, and forms weed-smothering clumps of gracefully arching, light to mid green blades that are attractive in themselves. They contribute bold, sculptural effects at the edge of borders, and give interesting contrasts of shape against neighbours of a more spreading habit.

The flowers are their crowning glory. They are held aloft in loose clusters on slender stems, generally from late spring to late summer, but sometimes into autumn. Lily-like and trumpet shaped, they open in an array of pleasantly warm to scorching hues, sometimes with lighter-coloured midribs on the petals, or contrasting throats.

They may be dainty, half-opened trumpets or large, widely-flared blooms, occasionally opening almost flat. Their shortness of life is redeemed by the daily addition of new, fresh flowers to replace the old, opening one after another over several weeks.

The continuous efforts of nurserymen to produce new delights for our gardens has resulted in there being a very wide choice of hybrids available today, covering a spectrum of warm to hot tints, from soft melon-pinks to vibrant oranges and rich reds. Some of the loveliest are yellow, in shades from clear, delicate lemon to deep, glowing gold. A few of the paler yellows have the additional virtue of being deliciously fragrant.

Remember that nurseries have to choose a necessarily limited selection from this enormous variety and you will have to shop around if you have set your heart on a particular variety.

Of the yellows, 'Golden

Harry Smith

The flowers of the daylily may be short-lived, but their sheer profusion, with new buds jostling the spent flowers for room, more than makes up for this. This variety is 'Golden Chimes'.

PLANT PROFILE

Suitable site and soil Daylilies enjoy full sun or light shade and fertile, moist soil.

Planting Plant between mid-autumn and mid-spring, adding plenty of manure or compost to the weed-free site. Group three, four or five together for a bright show in summer, planting about 45cm/18in apart (more for large varieties, less for dwarfs).

Cultivation and care Once planted, daylilies do not take kindly to further disturbance. Mulch in spring to help retain moisture, and water generously in dry weather. As they flower, deadhead regularly, then cut the faded flower stems almost to the ground level once flowering is finished. An annual feed with a general fertilizer can help them along.

Propagation Divide and replant the fleshy roots in mild weather between autumn and spring. This should not be done until the plants are a few years old, and is best when overcrowding makes it necessary anyway.

Pests and diseases Daylilies are generally trouble-free, but try to protect the young foliage emerging in spring from slugs and snails.

Chimes' is a great favourite, with a particularly graceful habit. Like most hybrids it reaches a height of some 75cm/30in, but has relatively small flowers of a rich golden hue, tinged brown on the reverse of the petals.

Another deep golden variety is 'Cartwheels', with large, bold, flowers that open almost flat. 'Corky' is a splendid dwarf form, about 45cm/18in tall. It flowers prolifically, with lemon-yellow trumpets, again brown on the reverse, borne in

All daylilies are at the warmer end of the colour spectrum, but some are more vibrant than others. The opulent, rosy pink flowers of 'Pink Damask' (right) verge on the pastel, while those of the aptly named 'Burning Daylight' (below right) are a flaming gold. The blooms of H. fulva *'Kwanzo Variegata' (below) are similarly coloured, and set off by leaves with a white stripe of variable width running down the centre.*

Photos Horticultural

Harry Smith

Eric Crichton

RECOMMENDED VARIETIES

You will be best rewarded if you can see the plants in flower before making your choice, since descriptions of colour can be very personal and may vary from nursery to nursery. Of the innumerable cultivated varieties available, try: 'Anzac' (red); 'Black Magic' (deep red); 'Bonanza' (orange with a darker centre); 'Burning Daylight' (deep orange); 'Cartwheels' (deep golden-yellow opening almost flat); 'Catherine Woodbury' (pink with a soft lime-green centre); 'Corky' (dwarf, lemon-yellow with brown backs); 'George Cunningham' (soft orange-pink with ruffled petals); 'Golden Chimes' (golden-yellow with brown backs); 'Golden Orchid', also known as 'Doubloon' (orange-yellow); 'Hyperion' (pure yellow); 'Luxury Lace' (lavender-pink with lime-green throats and almost white midribs); 'Pink Damask' (rose-pink with brownish-yellow throats); 'Stafford' (deep red with maroon and yellow throats and narrow yellow midribs); 'Stella de Oro' (dwarf, orange-yellow with green-tipped outer petals); 'Whichford' (primrose-yellow).

Of the species, try *Hemerocallis citrina* (large, fragrant lemon-yellow flowers); *H. dumortieri* (low-growing, golden-yellow with brown backs); tawny or fulvous daylily, *H. fulva* (tawny orange) – 'Kwanzo Variegata' has variable white stripes on the leaves, and 'Kwanzo Flore Pleno' has double flowers and bright young foliage; *H. lilio-asphodelus*, syn. *H. flava* (elegant habit, small lemon- or chrome-yellow flowers); and grass-leaved daylily, *H. minor* (low-growing, lemon-yellow with tawny backs).

Photos Horticultural

Harry Smith

branching sprays from late spring well into summer.

Taking over in midsummer and flowering on into autumn, 'Stella de Oro' is another dwarf form, growing to about 40cm/16in. Its abundant small flowers are more widely bell-shaped, a pale orange-yellow in colour with the outer petals tipped green.

Orange flowers add balance and harmony to hot planting schemes and look spectacular against a background of purple or bronze foliage. Try the lovely 'Burning Daylight', a deep orange, and 'Bonanza', a lighter shade but with a darker, almost maroon centre.

One of the best red varieties is the handsome 'Stafford', flowering from midsummer. Its deep red petals are enlivened with narrow, yellow midribs extending from a maroon and yellow throat.

Some of the pink forms have delightful variations in colour. 'Pink Damask' is clear rose-

Photos Horticultural

The dwarf form 'Stella de Oro' (above) sometimes has green tips to its outer petals. It may occasionally be offered for sale as 'Stella d'Oro'.

Bred more than 40 years ago, 'Black Magic' (above right) is a dark red, one of the deepest colours of any daylily, though not at all as dark as its varietal name suggests.

'Stafford' (left) comes close to rivalling 'Black Magic' in the richness of its red, but has an added attraction in the yellow midrib which runs from its throat down the centre of each petal.

The species form of the tawny daylily (H. fulva, right) has less showy flowers than most of the hybrids derived from it, but compensates for this in the vigour of its growth, soon forming a clump around 75cm/ 30in across.

Andrew Lawson

pink with a brownish-yellow throat, while the curled and ruffled petals of 'Luxury Lace' are a soft lavender-pink with almost white midribs, opening from late summer to reveal lime-green throats.

Original species

The species from which the innumerable modern hybrids were originally raised are also well worth growing, though are often harder to find.

The fulvous or tawny daylily (*Hemerocallis fulva*) is the source of many of the modern varieties. It is vigorous in growth, reaching 1m/3ft tall and a spread of some 75cm/ 30in. From mid to late summer it carries tawny-orange flowers. The variety 'Kwanzo Variegata' is unusual in that its leaves are marked with a broad white stripe, though this can vary in its appearance. 'Kwanzo Flore Pleno' has bright young foliage and fragrant, double, dusky-orange trumpet-shaped blooms.

One of the earliest-flowering daylilies is *H. lilio-asphodelus* (syn. *H. flava*). Though robust and spreading, it is smaller – about 60cm/2ft in height – with slender leaves, and a more elegant habit than most daylilies. Delicate, fragrant flowers of a clear lemon or chrome yellow open in succession for 6-8 weeks from the end of spring.

There are low-growing species, too. *H. dumortieri* achieves a compact 45cm/18in, bearing fragrant, golden-

The startling flowers of 'Doubloon' (below), with their narrow, elongated petals, are closer to those of orchids than lilies, a resemblance reflected in the variety's other name, 'Golden Orchid'.

Eric Crichton

Photos Horticultural

yellow flowers with tawny-brown backs. The grass-leaved daylily (*H. minor*) is a little smaller, with fragrant, lemon-yellow flowers encircled by tawny-backed outer petals.

Adaptable plants

Daylilies are quite tough plants, happy in any good, moist garden soil, in sun or light shade, and little troubled by pests and diseases. They give their best show when planted in small drifts rather than individually, so group four or five together.

Once planted, in autumn or spring, they respond best to being left undisturbed for a few years, except for regular deadheading to encourage flowering, and the subsequent cutting back of spent flower stems. Once frosts take hold, the dying leaves can look untidy, but they can provide

The profuse yellow blooms of 'Cartwheels' (left) have a much flatter profile than most other daylilies, resembling stars rather than trumpets.

'George Cunningham' (right) is distinguished both by its lovely, delicate, pale apricot colouring and by its handsomely ruffled petals.

Photos Horticultural

PERFECT PARTNERS

Mix together yellow and blue-flowering plants for a refreshingly cool display in the heat of summer. Mingle yellow daylilies and chrysanthemums with the blues of agapanthus, lavender, *Anchusa azurea*, *Polemonium foliosissimum* and geraniums such as 'Johnson's Blue'. Make sure the colours sit easily together by mixing like with like, placing softer blues with the paler yellows.

As daylilies are happy on acid soils, and have roughly the same tonal range, they can also be used to underplant azaleas (right) and rhododendrons.

Both pink and orange daylilies will give a striking show against purple or bronze foliage. Appropriate neighbours might be *Cotinus coggygria* 'Royal Purple' or 'Notcutt's Variety', *Acer palmatum* 'Atropurpureum' or *Berberis thunbergii atropurpurea*.

Harry Smith

important protection for the dormant plants over the winter months.

Because the young plants dislike disturbance, you should put off increasing your stock until overcrowding makes it necessary. Daylilies can be invasive, so dividing the tuberous roots every few years can be useful for control as well as propagation.

Planting times

Choose mild weather between mid-autumn and mid-spring for the task. Carefully lift the clump, shake off any loose material and dunk the roots in a bucket of water to wash away the soil and make your work much easier. The growth buds of daylilies are in the crown of fleshy roots, so cut downwards through the clump, dividing it into several pieces, each with a few growth buds. The divisions should be planted straight away to the same depth as they were before lifting.

79

➤─┤─◆❭─◗─❬◆─┤─◄

Success with
Bulbs, Corms and Tubers

Bulbs, corms, rhizomes and tubers are types of food storage organs developed by plants for their survival from one growing season to the next.

Onions, daffodils, tulips and fritillarias all grow from bulbs. A bulb is a modified shoot, with its very short stem enclosed by layers of fleshy leaves.

In the first year of a bulbous plant, the food manufactured by the leaves is moved to the base of each leaf. These bases become the fleshy layers of the bulb. They are the part of the onion that we eat.

The following year, a bud within the bulb springs into life and produces new leaves, which in turn make food and store it in their bases.

Once the bulb is large enough (and the exact size depends on the plant) a flower bud is produced and this grows in the following year.

Corms

Corms are swollen stem bases. Examples are crocus, freesia and gladiolus. The first year's leaves make and then transport food down the stem to form a corm.

This lies dormant until the next growing period, when the terminal bud uses the stored food to grow. The roots then develop and flowers and leaves are produced.

More manufactured food is transported to the bottom of the stem where a new corm is formed on top of the old one, which eventually shrivels. Cormlets (small corms) are also produced. These can be separated from the parent corm and replanted.

Rhizomes

A rhizome is an underground stem which does not necessarily store food. Examples of food-storing rhizomes include iris

Photos Horticultural

The white flowers of Ornithogalum nutans (above) grow from bulbs.

At near left is a bulb, then two tubers, three corms and two more tubers (right).

Bulbils (mini-bulbs) grow from the stems of lilies and the onion family (top).

Peter McHoy

PROPAGATION

You can increase your stocks by digging up congested clumps, teasing the growth apart and replanting them at a better spacing. Bulbs should be teased apart, as should corms.

Rhizomes grow outwards, which leaves old growth in the middle of the clump. Dig up and chop off the outer pieces for replanting. Discard the central section.

If leaves are attached to new sections of rhizome, cut them down to half their original height, to prevent the wind dislodging the newly planted piece.

Propagate bulbs and corms once the foliage has died back; iris after flowering.

and arum. The leaves manufacture food which is transported to the rhizome and to any lateral buds.

The main rhizome increases in length each year. One or more branches may develop off it and they, too, will grow longer. In spring, food is transferred to aerial shoots which develop into the plant's new leaves and flowers.

Tubers

A tuber is a thickened, fleshy underground root (as in the dahlia) or stem (a potato, for example), which helps the plant survive periods of cold or drought. Many popular plants have tubers, including arum lilies, dahlias and many types of begonias.

Once the plant is dormant, the tubers can be lifted and cut up, with at least one 'eye' or bud on each piece, which is then replanted.

Planting depth

As a rule of thumb, plant bulbs, corms and tubers at least twice as deep as their diameter. Gardening books give detailed information about particular species.

Some plants which are not completely frost-hardy have a better chance of survival if buried deeper than the rule of thumb suggests. Further insulation can be provided by mulching the ground.

Rhizomes are not usually planted as deep as bulbs and

Peter McHoy

corms. Iris rhizomes are planted very shallowly, with their tops visible on the soil's surface, so that the sun can ripen each year's growth.

What to lift

You only need to dig up (lift) bulbs, corms, rhizomes or tubers if they are not winter-hardy. They should be brought into a frost-free place to ensure survival. The only other time to lift them is when dividing and replanting (see box).

However, garden tulips (but not species tulips) benefit from being lifted and moved to another part of the garden each year, in order to prevent disease problems.

The other situation where you may want to lift bulbs, corms, rhizomes or tubers is where you grow spring and summer bedding plants. When you pull up the spring bedding to make way for the summer plants, the bulb foliage may still be present, or the bulbs may be too near the surface for you to plant above them.

In this situation, you can lift all the bulbs, but you must replant them elsewhere straight away, so that they can complete their growth cycle and die back naturally. Otherwise the bulbs will not receive a top-up of nutrients and next year's flower bud may not form.

Bulbs, corms, rhizomes and tubers are liable to damage and drying out, so try to buy

them as soon as they are delivered, healthy and intact, to the shop or garden centre.

Avoid shrivelled up material (but remember that corms are often very dry and shrivelled). Do not buy very soft, bruised or otherwise damaged material. Also to be avoided are those with shoots or roots.

Replanting

Bulbs, corms, rhizomes and tubers are sold in a dry state for convenience. You can, though, dig up and replant them while they are in leaf, providing that you do not allow the roots to dry out.

In fact, snowdrops are more successfully established 'in the green' – that is, with their leaves on. Specialist nurseries sell these by mail order or you can beg some from friends. Wait until the flowers are over, because the flowers will wilt if you move them and you will not have the pleasure of their display.

Snowdrop bulbs dry out too much indoors, which is why shop-bought bulbs are often unsuccessful. Grape hyacinth

Andrew Lawson

PLANTS FOR DRY SHADE

Name	Type	Flower
Chionodoxa luciliae	Bulb	Spring, blue
Colchicum speciosum		
Meadow saffron	Corm	Autumn, pink, purple, white
Corydalis solida	Tuber	Spring, purple
Crocus tommasinianus		
Crocus	Corm	Early spring, lilac
Cyclamen hederifolium		
Cyclamen	Tuber	Autumn, pink
Eranthis hyemalis		
Winter aconite	Tuber	Early spring, yellow
Galanthus nivalis Snowdrop	Bulb	Early spring, white
Hyacinthoides non-scriptus		
English bluebell	Bulb	Late spring, blue
Narcissus pseudonarcissus		
Wild daffodil	Bulb	Spring, yellow
Ornithogalum nutans	Bulb	Spring, white
Scilla bifolia Squill	Bulb	Spring, blue

PLANTS FOR VERY MOIST SOIL IN SHADE

Name	Type	Flower
Allium siculum	Bulb	Early summer, purple/green
Camassia leichtlinii Quamash	Bulb	Early summer, blue
Lilium pardalinum Panther lily	Bulb	Summer, red/orange
Lilium superbum Swamp lily	Bulb	Summer, red/orange
Trillium spp	Rhizome	Spring, various

Eric Crichton

(*Muscari* spp) bulbs are also prone to drying out so they should be bought soon after being delivered to the shop. These are not often sold 'in the green', but they are so common in gardens that you can probably beg some from a friend.

Growing conditions

Those bulbs, corms, rhizomes and tubers that need full sun require it in order to ripen and produce good growth and flowers the following year. Few will tolerate extremely dry soil, however.

Moisture is necessary to start them into growth and to help elongate the flower stalks of the taller types. You may have noticed how a clump of daffodils produces shorter flower stalks in dry years.

Our spring-flowering bulbs are adapted to grow in woods. They thrive because they complete their growth before the trees begin theirs. The trees are still dormant when the bulbs need moisture. Sun and rain can penetrate to the ground because the trees' leaves are not yet open. By the time the full leaf canopy is out, the ground level show is over.

A garden is less natural. It often has evergreen trees, hedges and shrubs, which are a barrier to sun and rain and are competing for moisture.

Eric Crichton

Several of our most popular spring flowers grow from bulbs. They include bluebells (left) and daffodils (below left).

Iris rhizomes (opposite bottom) are usually divided and planted out after flowering. They can take a time to become established and often do not flower until the second season.

After lifting in autumn these gladioli corms (below) must be dried out before being stored in a cool, frost-free place.

PLANTS FOR FULL SUN

Name	Type	Flower
Agapanthus African blue lily	Tuber	Summer, blue
Allium aflatunense	Bulb	Late spring, pink/purple
Allium moly Golden garlic	Bulb	Late spring, yellow
Arum spp	Tuber	Spring, yellow or black
Brodiaea spp	Bulb	Late spring, blue/violet
Gladioli Gladiolus	Corm	Summer, various
Hyacinth Hyacinth	Bulb	Spring, various
Iris spp Iris	Rhizome or bulb	Spring, summer, various
Nerine spp	Bulb	Autumn, pink
Oxalis spp (most) Sorrel	Rhizome or tuber	Late spring, various
Tulipa spp and hybrids Tulip	Bulb	Spring, various

Collections/Patrick Johns

PLANTS TO LIFT BEFORE FROSTS

Name	Type
Agapanthus spp (hybrids are hardy) African blue lily	Tuber
Anomatheca laxa Lapeirousia	Corm
Caladium spp Angel's wings	Tuber
Chlidanthus fragrans Perfumed fairy lily	Bulb
Clivia spp Kaffir lily	Rhizome
Eucomis spp Pineapple lily	Bulb
Freesia spp Freesia	Corm
Gladioli Gladiolus	Corm
Haemanthus spp Blood lily	Bulb
Iris orchioides one of the Juno irises	Bulb
Sauromatum venosum Voodoo lily	Tuber
Sparaxis tricolor Harlequin flower	Corm
Tigridia pavonia Tiger flower	Bulb
Tritonia spp Tritonia	Corm
Watsonia spp Bugle lily	Corm
Zantedeschia spp Arum lily	Tuber

To naturalize bulbs in grass or woods plant them in random groups and singly.

When planting in flower beds, plant them near other plants which will grow up and disguise the bulb foliage when it is dying back. You can also plant them beneath deciduous shrubs and among shrubs with a short flowering season, to brighten up a dull area.

Sources of bulbs

The demand for bulbs, corms, rhizomes and tubers from gardeners has resulted in wild populations of plants being robbed. Although garden hybrids are bred and grown by commercial nurseries, species such as cyclamen, snowdrop and snowflake may not be.

Unfortunately, once dug up from the wild, they are not kept for propagation, but sold. This is happening particularly in Turkey. If possible, buy stock from cultivated plants of endangered species such as cyclamen.

Make sure that the soil in which you plant the bulbs will be moist (but well-drained) at the critical growing time.

You may have to add garden compost to the planting area to increase moisture retention. Water the area well in order to encourage growth.

Many bulbs, corms, rhizomes and tubers, such as anemones, can be started off by soaking them before planting. If you soak the ground, too, they will have a good chance of becoming established.

Plant bulbs in clumps for a splash of colour, or plant them in drifts to flower through other plants or between rocks.

WHEN TO PLANT

Spring: summer-flowering bulbs.

Early autumn: madonna lilies, colchicums, autumn-flowering crocus, daffodils, winter aconites and snowdrops.

Late autumn: tulips.

Brilliant Blooms

**Fill every spare inch of your garden with summer
bedding plants and their vibrant colours will provide
a glorious display for months.**

Andrew Lawson

Most of us have a limited amount of time to spend in the garden, and this is where summer bedding plants can be such a boon to today's busy gardener. To make the most of them, plant them together in generous clusters to create a bold splash of colour rather than space them out along a border where the eye-catching effect of their colour will be lost. The hard work has already been done by somebody else so these half-hardy annuals, raised from seed in their containers, save you all the bother of providing heat and light, and of pricking-out and hardening-off. All you have to do is go to your nearest garden centre or market – or even a large supermarket – in early summer when sudden frosts are less likely, choose what you like, and plant it immediately. The result should be a display of massed brilliance which will last until the very end of the summer.

No trouble

If your garden is still at the early planning stage, you should leave half-circles, at least 45cm/18in deep, between other plants. Of course, the width very much depends on the size of your garden: if you have a very small garden, you will not want large areas left bare until the summer.

One solution for the spring and autumn months would be to grow small bulbs in these spaces. Use a trowel rather than a fork when planting out your bedding plants to avoid accidentally damaging the bulbs below the soil.

If you already have shrubs which are planted close together, with little room for anything else in between, you may need to move them. The best time to do this is in the autumn when they are dormant. If you want 'pockets' of flowers among your shrubs immediately cut shrubs back slightly. Few resent a little gentle pruning at the wrong time. Do remember, though, that their already established roots will take up any food you provide so water and feed the new arrivals very carefully.

Cheap and cheerful

The cheapest and most efficient way to buy bedding plants is in 'snap-off' strips of plastic or polystyrene. Each full set should contain around 10 annuals such as petunia, and the roots suffer less than they do in trays packed with around 40 plants where you have to prise more roots apart before you can safely plant them.

Never buy plants which are in full flower, and avoid lanky stems, discoloured leaves or any plants that have been reduced in price – these will not produce the best results. You should also avoid anything that has simply been lifted directly out of the ground and wrapped in newspaper.

Bright and bushy

Turn containers upside-down to make sure the roots are not growing through the bottom. Pick out plants that have good, strong stems with leaves near the base. Make sure they are bushy and are not packed closely, that they are all about the same size, and that the compost is moist.

A final word of warning about buying: quite a few growers, anxious to attract those who want something different, have bred spots and stripes into what were once self-coloured plants. These can look dramatic in a bed of their own in a large garden or in containers, but can be overpowering when grown in a small space with other plants,

Harry Smith Collection

Bedding plants can transform even the smallest garden (above). The pretty dazzling white fence contrasts brightly with the reds, yellows, greens and pinks of the flowers. Begonias, fuchsias and salvias offer interesting contrasts in shape and texture as well as colour.

GARDEN NOTES

HARDY OR HALF-HARDY?

Q What is the difference between 'hardy' and 'half-hardy'?

A Hardy plants are those which are able to thrive outdoors all year round. Half-hardy plants will live outside only in summer, until the first frosts kill them.

so bear this in mind when choosing what to buy.

When you get your new purchases home, plant them immediately without worrying about your soil type as bedding plants are not fussy about where they live though many of them do well only in full sun. Now all you have to do is water them in and feed them – and sit back to await exclamations of amazement from friends and family who visit your garden.

Pretty popular

The following are the easiest and most popular half-hardies. Approximate heights are given to help the beginner plan the bed, but do not worry about spacing between them just mass the plants together.

African marigolds grow up to 3ft, though there are also dwarf varieties available.

A garden bursting at the seams with bright summer bedding can look absolutely spectacular. In this garden (left) bedding plants in pinks and white have been massed together to produce an explosion of colour.

Bedding plants in a wide range of colours contrast happily in this border (right). Buy them by the trayful as small plants and plant them where you want them to grow. Plant in groups rather than singly. The display will be blooming in no time and the beauty of it is that all the hard work has been done for you – no need to fuss over pricking out seedlings and hardening off.

J.S. Sira/Garden Picture Library

If you stick to one colour the effect can be very pretty but you can stick to one family and still achieve a varied display. All the yellow plants (left) are tagetes (marigolds). The tallest are 'Lemon Gem', the middle are 'Inca' and the small blooms are 'Primrose Lady'.

A display of mixed petunias in purple, cerise and white (above) can create a delightfully simple effect. They are also good for containers.

be staked. The best type for general use are 'short' antirrhinums, which reach a height of about 22cm/9in. Mixed antirrhinums can be an astonishing sight, requiring little else for summer brilliance in small gardens – but the whole display can be ruined by an outbreak of rust disease. To avoid a season of disappointment, it is best to buy your plants from a reliable garden centre, and ask for rust-resistant varieties. Sometimes the plants last through

They have attractive, scented leaves in a range from pale yellow to deep orange.

Ageratum is also known as floss flower, and 'Blue Mink' is probably the most popular variety. Reaching a height of 20-25cm/8-10in, it produces fluffy blue flowers throughout

the summer and into early autumn. It also looks good when grown in containers with pretty white petunias.

Alyssum is a popular edging plant. The white varieties are best for this purpose because they provide a good contrast to a backdrop of taller, brilliantly coloured plants. Only 7-15cm/3-6in high, it tends to self-seed for the following year. You often see white alyssum combined with blue lobelia, in neat alternating clumps in a border. This can produce a rather regimented look, however, so avoid it if you want to create an effect of natural abundance.

Antirrhinum is commonly known as snapdragon. There are four sizes, ranging from 'dwarf', which are ideal for rockeries, to 'tall', that need to

GROWING TIPS

ALMOST INSTANT

Always keep a couple of packets of seeds – mixed cornflowers, pot marigolds (calendula) and mixed candytuft. Then, if anything fails, or if you find that you did not buy enough, you can still get almost instant colour. All you have to do is sow them thinly straight into the ground exactly as you want to see them grow. Cover them lightly and keep them moist.

PERFECT PARTNERS

the winter, but to avoid spreading any disease, it is best to remove them entirely after flowering.

Asters may have a short life, but the ones you can buy in early summer can do a lot to add a touch of colour to a drab corner. Available in attractive colours, these reach a height of 15cm/6in.

More favourites

Begonia semperflorens is a must in any bedding display. With red, pink or white flowers, often bronze-coloured foliage, and growing only about 17cm/7in tall, these well-tempered plants will brighten dull corners, tubs, window boxes and hanging baskets and do not even mind shade. It is best not to mix begonias with other brightly coloured half-hardies, as they will detract from each other. Use them in clumps in the border, as edging, or around miniature conifers in tubs.

Canterbury bell is a popular biennial which flowers for only three months and needs supporting. But, if you have room for it, by all means buy it

Bedding plants need not be planted in a mass. You can use them selectively just to pick out some features of your garden design. These dwarf busy Lizzies (right) are surrounding a pond, bringing life and colour to an otherwise dull stone edging. Although you may not normally match pink and red, with bedding plants anything goes!

LONGER LIFE

When frosts are forecast, do not desert your begonias or busy Lizzies because, with your help, they will continue to flower indoors all winter. Dig them up with a reasonable amount of soil attached and pot them up in soil-less compost in a pot just a little larger then the root ball. Snip out any withered, rotten, dead or diseased stems and trim the rest over lightly.

Brian Carter/Garden Picture Library

Photos Horticultural

For a vivid contrast, fill a whole bed, or at least a large area, with a generous patch of shiny begonia semperflorens dotted with

iresine (left).
Vivid purple heliotrope and silver-leaved senecio (above) are edged with a frame of geraniums.

for its attractive looks – perhaps in blue and white for a cottage garden look. It can grow to 90cm/3ft tall. Shorter varieties are available for rockeries, but these still need support.

Impatiens, or busy Lizzie, is the kind of good-natured, free-flowering plant that every busy gardener needs. Many people think of it only as a house plant, but gardeners have now seen its many advantages and are including it in the flower border. It will cheerfully go anywhere – under trees, in shady beds, in full sun – and will produce continual displays of brilliant colour. Its only disadvantage is that it needs a lot of watering. Busy Lizzie is available in many forms – plain, bi-colour, single, double, and even with variegated foliage. It reaches

about 15-23cm/6-9in tall, but has a drooping habit rather than remaining upright. One plastic 'strip' of perfectly plain plants is particularly useful for a tub on the patio, if your view from the sitting-room needs a bit of a lift in summer.

Lovely lobelia

Lobelia is probably most popular in its blue forms, and blue remains the favourite colour for edging flower beds or trailing from window boxes, hanging baskets or patio pots. Lobelia is a small plant, only growing to a height of 10cm/4in. If there is a bit of soil under the trailing varieties, you may find that they have seeded themselves and will flower again next year. They are especially useful for filling out hanging baskets, window boxes or containers, and can

look particularly lovely with just one other colour such as a pink ivy-leaved pelargonium (geranium).

Nemesia lasts for only a couple of months – much less than other annuals – but it would be a pity not to buy any because the mixed colours are so beautiful. The plants will tolerate light shade but, since they do not take kindly to a lot

of lime in the soil, you could use them with success on a patio in pots full of ericaceous compost. They grow about 25cm/10in tall, and should be cut back a little when the first flush of flowering is over.

Nicotiana (tobacco plant) smells marvellous on warm, romantic summer evenings. Some varieties close up during the day, but growers also pro-

Brilliant blooms transform a window box (above) and guarantee that the view from the window will be lovely. Lobelia, petunias and geraniums are used.

Take bedding plants to new heights with hanging baskets (below). Use geraniums, begonias and nasturtiums.

duce small varieties, with bright little faces, that remain open. These have no perfume, however, so are best avoided if you particularly want a touch of scent in your border. If you want that irresistible scent, then look for tall plants with white or pale green flowers; these produce rather straggly growth, though, so tuck them at the back of your bed.

Perfect pelargoniums

Pelargoniums, or geraniums, make excellent summer bedding and will overwinter indoors for next year. You can take cuttings from them very easily, too, and increase your stock further for a really colourful show. They grow to about 60cm/24in and come in white, pinks and reds, with many bi-coloured flowers and variegated or scented leaves.

Petunias are available in both striped and self-coloured forms. Stick to the latter if you mix them with other colourful bedders. They grow to about 20cm/8in and quite enjoy dry weather. The colours are wonderful, the flowers profuse, and the plants do not resent being gently chopped back if they become too straggly. They also propagate very easily.

Summer bedding plants (facing page) are planted en masse, bringing colour and vibrancy.

Water Lilies

Aquatic aristocrats, water lilies are breathtakingly beautiful. They are often regarded as difficult to grow but they are easy, even if you don't have a pond.

Derek Gould

The very name water lily conjures images of beauty and elegance, and even the Latin name has romantic and graceful overtones: *Nymphaea* means water nymph.

The roots of these water plants embed themselves in the mud at the bottom of the pond (or in the soil in their planting containers). From these strong roots grows a thick root stock, topped with leaves and flowers that float gracefully on the surface.

As a family, water lilies are surprisingly varied. Some have blue flowers that stand

Water lilies are easy to grow and quick to multiply. N. 'Chromatella' (above top), has an exquisite, delicate shape and a beautiful, translucent yellow colour.

above the water; others are so small you can grow them in a tiny sink garden. Their large, flat leaves, which float on the surface of the water, provide shade for fish and help to inhibit the growth of algae.

Variegated and scented varieties are popular today and long ago there were even some which were regarded as an edible delicacy. The ancient Egyptians pounded the seeds and roots to make a bread or would eat the roots both raw and cooked. In Australia they were eaten by aborigines. Different parts of these plants have also been used medicinally and as an aphrodisiac.

Cures for cold

All the hardy water lilies mentioned here will survive cold winters, but take care if you are planting them in very shallow ponds as the roots must be below the ice to survive if the pond freezes over. You are unlikely to lose any water lilies planted in 30cm/12in or more of water.

Dwarf and miniature varieties grown in raised containers should be moved to a more sheltered spot or even indoors during severe cold spells. Plants left in a pond will certainly be damaged if the water freezes solid.

Tropical water lilies can be grown outside as long as they are brought indoors for the winter months. Lift the roots and plant them in moist sand in a cool, sheltered place that escapes the frost.

When to plant

The best time to plant the hardy kinds is when the first young leaves appear, but any time from early spring to early summer is suitable. Tropical kinds, however, should not be planted out until later in the summer.

You can plant lilies directly into soil in the bottom of the pond or container, but it is generally more convenient to plant them in special plastic

PLANT PROFILE
NYMPHAEA (WATER LILY)

Suitable site and soil: In ornamental pools, in a fertile, loamy soil.

Cultivation and care: They require little attention after planting, though they may need thinning occasionally. This is best done in spring.

Propagation: Divide roots or remove young offsets. Insert in small pots filled with loam, stand in a bowl, fill with water to 1.5 cm/½in above pot rim and leave in full sun until well rooted, before planting out into permanent position.

Pests and diseases: Leaves may attract water lily beetle (although this is rare). Leaves and flowers attract aphids. Insects can simply be hosed off. Leaf spot (pale brown circles of fungus) and stem rot (blackened stems) are more serious. Remove affected leaves and/or stems.

Under the surface: It is just as important to know what is going on under water. Different types of water lily grow to different heights, so it is important to choose a variety suitable for the depth of your pond. The tuber-like rhizomes are planted in the mud of the pond's bottom, or in containers or baskets placed at different heights in the water, usually on especially raised surfaces. Some varieties are more vigorous than others and may need to be thinned out every 2-3 years by dividing the rhizomes.

'Mrs. Richmond' (above) has perfectly flat leaves and succulent pink flowers. Lifting their faces to the sun on elegant long necks this fragrant 'Director Moore' flower (left) has a sunny yellow centre. The brilliant red water lily 'Escarboucle' (below) sits in striking contrast on flat, circular, deepest green leaves.

Peter McHoy

RECOMMENDED VARIETIES

The first process of selection is to find the variety of water lily most suitable for the size of your pond or container. Then decide on the particular colour you would like.

Planting depth is the depth of water above the soil or compost level – not to the bottom of the pond. The depth is only a guide as some of the miniatures will grow in just a few inches of water while others will happily tolerate 30cm/12in deeper than indicated.

Although some of those lilies listed are species (*N. candida* for example) others are hybrids and you often find them listed on plant labels and in catalogues as 'varieties'.

For a dish, sink or tub

Planting depth 10-23cm/4-9in

- *N. candida* (white)
- *N. pygmaea* 'Alba' (white)
- *N. pygmaea* 'Helvola' (yellow)

For a small pond

Planting depth 15-30cm/6-12in

- 'Froebeli' (deep red, free-flowering and fragrant)
- 'Laydekeri Purpurata' (masses of flowers over a long season, wine red pointed petals and leaves splashed with maroon)
- 'William Falconer' (dark red)
- 'Odorata Minor' (white, scented, suitable for a tub as well as a small pool)
- 'Paul Hariot' (opens pale yellow, then deepens to copper-red; fragrant)
- 'Rose Arey' (large pink flowers; very fragrant)

For a large pond

Planting depth 23-45cm/9-18in

- 'Albatross' (white)
- 'Director Moore' (light green leaves, purple flowers with yellow centres, tropical type)
- 'Laydekeri Lilacea' (pink and fragrant)
- 'James Brydon' (crimson, peony-shaped flowers and leaves flecked with maroon)
- 'Marliacea Chromatella' (yellow and slightly fragrant)
- 'Mme Wilfron Gonnère' (pink)
- 'Odorata Alba' (white, cup-shaped and fragrant)
- 'Renée Gerard' (pink, blotched and splashed crimson towards centre)

Tania Midgley

N. pygmaea 'Helvola' (above) has small olive-green leaves and star shaped flowers. N. Froebelii (left) is a deep pink lily with mottled leaves.

The reddish tinged leaves and pink flowers are typical of 'Rose Arey' (below). 'James Brydon' (bottom) has fragrant crimson flowers.

Peter McHoy

Pat Brindley

pond baskets available from garden centres. Line these baskets with squares of hessian to prevent the soil falling through. An old plastic washing basket will do the job just as well. The advantage of planting in a container is that it is much easier to lift out the container than to cope with fleshy roots that have penetrated the whole pond.

Nurseries that specialize in aquatic plants sell heavy loam, but ordinary garden soil is perfectly adequate. Avoid soil that has been enriched with powerful chemical fertilizers or manure, however, as this will encourage the invasive growth of algae in the pond. Mix in a handful of bone meal, or add a sachet of special slow-release fertilizer sold for aquatic plants.

Growing tips

To reduce the amount of clouding that occurs when you first immerse the container in water, cover the surface of the

POTENTIAL PESTS

You can grow water lilies for years and never have any problems, but there are a couple of pests of which you should beware.

- *Water lily aphids* are like the common blackfly that you may find in other parts of the garden. Do not spray them with an insecticide – you will harm other wildlife and fish in the pond. Just hose the pests off and let the fish eat them.
- *Water lily beetles* are fortunately rare. The shiny black larvae with yellow undersides and the small dark brown beetles severely damage the leaves, which then start to rot. Pick off and destroy badly affected leaves; otherwise hose the insects off.

GO ORGANIC!

Peter McHoy

GROWING TIPS

INCREASING YOUR INVESTMENT

Divison is the simplest way of raising water lilies. Lift the roots in late spring and remove some of the 'branches' from the original root. Provided they have a healthy shoot at the end, they should grow. Place in loam-filled pots or simply replant them straight into the pond.

container with a thick layer of gravel. If the water lilies are going in a pond, this will also deter the fish from stirring up the soil in the container. Instead of plunging the container directly into the pond, it is best to lower it over a period of time as the leaf stems elongate. Rest the container on a few bricks initially and remove them in stages, as the plants begin to grow.

The only requirement for good flowering is a sunny position. Provided you choose a variety suitable for your size of pond and depth of water, hardy water lilies will flower well, the number of blooms increasing after the first year or two.

You do not even need a pond

Make a wonderful table centrepiece by growing a miniature water lily in a bowl. The roots are planted in a smaller dish in a complimentary colour. This pink hued lily makes a striking contrast with the black bowl.

Water plants are sometimes sold separately in garden centres and nurseries, from early spring to early summer. They are also available by mail from water plant specialists. Check the mature size before you buy as some varieties spread very quickly.

Derek Gould

CUT FLOWERS

One of the drawbacks of water lilies is that they can be rather inaccessible and you may have to get down on your knees to enjoy their scent. Try cutting a few and floating them on water in a dish indoors; many will last for days.

A BUYER'S GUIDE

Popular varieties are available from most good garden centres from early spring to early summer. Outside the main planting season you may be able to obtain them from water garden specialists.

If you do not have a stockist in your area, you can buy them by mail from water plant specialists. New or rare old varieties can be expensive but most are relatively cheap. Beware though of any not listed here that seem very cheap – they may be very vigorous varieties which will quickly invade small ponds.

PROJECT   A SUNKEN BARREL POND FOR WATER LILIES

Michael Shoebridge

Naturalize the sunken barrel by surrounding it with large pebbles and gravel. This will also serve as a safety measure and will prevent the careless from stumbling into it! If you have small children it will be safer not to sink the barrel, but to leave it free standing.

Sink a watertight half barrel into a hole so that it fits snuggly. Use a spirit level to make sure that it is horizontal. Put a 7.5cm/3in layer of loam or good garden soil in the bottom. Part fill the tub with water. Plant the water lilies. *N. pygmaea* 'Alba' is a good choice for a small tub as it is hardy and small, yet produces a

stunning display of bright yellow flowers. Allow the water to settle before adding a layer of gravel to anchor the plant. Finally top up the water to a total depth of 22-30cm/9-12in. You are likely to lose lilies in bad weather if the water is too shallow. Divide plants in years to come to prevent the tub becoming overcrowded.

to grow the smaller ones. The true miniatures such as 'Helvola' can be grown in a small dish on a windowsill or in an old sink. The most compact varieties of the larger types, such as 'Froebeli' are perfect for small barrels – try sinking them to the rim in the ground, then plant a lily in each one.

Index

*P*hotographic *C*redits

ANDREW LAWSON *12, 13, 15, 35, 39, 44, 52, 67, 77, 82, 84*
COLLECTIONS *23, 30, 65, 68, 83, 88*; DAVID SQUIRE *16, 66*
DEREK GOULD *7, 84, 90, 93*; DON WILDRIDGE *10, 53*
ERIC CRICHTON *13, 32, 37, 44, 46, 58, 61, 63, 64, 75, 78, 82*
GARDEN PICTURE LIBRARY *17, 21, 22, 28, 45, 48, 54, 56, 59, 62, 63, 85, 86, 87*; Gillian Beckett *29, 38, 49, 51, 57*
HARRY SMITH COLLECTION *7, 8, 9, 14, 19, 32, 33, 37, 40, 43, 45, 59, 61, 63, 69, 70, 71, 73, 74, 75, 76, 79, 85, 86, 88*
INSIGHT PICTURE LIBRARY *33, 49, 56*; JOHN GLOVER *29, 55*; MARSHALL CAVENDISH *24*
NEIL HOLMES *47*; NHPA *47*; PAT BRINDLEY *12, 13, 34, 39, 51, 56, 57, 58, 92*; PAUL FELIX *18*
PETER McHOY *11, 15, 25, 26, 29, 35, 37, 42, 72, 80, 81, 89, 91, 92, 93*
PHOTOS HORTICULTURAL *6, 8, 10, 14, 18, 23, 24, 25, 27, 28, 30, 40, 41, 50, 52, 57, 60, 64, 67, 69,*
70, 72, 75, 76, 77, 78, 79, 80, 86, 87, 91; RAY DAVIS *59*
S & O MATHEWS *40, 54*; SIMON HAY *20*; SUSIE JOHNS *20*
TANIA MIDGLEY *9, 15, 31, 32, 34, 36, 50, 53, 54, 66, 71, 92*